ISLAM

A MOSAIC, NOT A MONOLITH

ISLAM

A MOSAIC, NOT A MONOLITH

VARTAN GREGORIAN

BROOKINGS INSTITUTION PRESS
Washington, D.C.

Copyright © 2003 by Carnegie Corporation of New York

All rights reserved. No part of this publication may be reproduced or transmitted in any form or by any means without permission in writing from the Brookings Institution Press, 1775 Massachusetts Avenue, N.W., Washington, D.C. 20036 (fax: 202/797-6195 or e-mail: permissions@brookings.edu).

The Library of Congress has cataloged the hardcover edition as follows:
Gregorian, Vartan.
    Islam : a mosaic, not a monolith / Vartan Gregorian.
        p.   cm.
Includes bibliographical references and index.
    ISBN 0-8157-3282-1
    1. Islamic countries—Politics and government—20th century.   2. Islam and politics—Islamic countries.   3. Islamic renewal—Islamic countries.
    4. Nationalism—Islamic countries—History—20th century.   I. Title.
    DS35.77.G74 2003
    320.917'671—dc21   2003006189

ISBN 0-8157-3283-x (pbk. : alk. paper)

2 4 6 8 9 7 5 3 1

The paper used in this publication meets minimum requirements of the American National Standard for Information Sciences—Permanence of Paper for Printed Library Materials: ANSI Z39.48-1992.

Typeset in Minion

Composition by R. Lynn Rivenbark
Macon, Georgia

Printed by R. R. Donnelley
Harrisonburg, Virginia

CONTENTS

PREFACE

WHEN I ASSUMED the presidency of Carnegie Corporation of New York in 1997, I was concerned that our nation did not know very much about its own Muslim communities or even Islam, which is believed to be the fastest growing religion in the United States as well as in the world. I was concerned—in light of our growing Muslim population—that unless we knew and understood the true nature of Islam as a faith, our ethnic and race relations, and occasional tensions therein, would assume a religious character, thus increasing and complicating efforts to achieve tolerance within the American polity.

In reviewing Carnegie Corporation's priorities and future course of action, it became imperative to address this issue. Initially, the corporation held two conferences, which were attended by scholars and some Muslim American leaders. The meetings focused on the enormous diversity within the American Muslim community and the complex nature of Islam. In addition, participants discussed some of the inherent conflicts that immigrants in general, and Muslim immigrants in particular, must resolve to become an integral part of the social fabric of the United States.

Two major themes emerged: the need to promote public understanding about the rich legacy and diversity of Islam and the need to ease the integration of Muslim citizens into U.S. society and encourage their participation in its democracy. The achievement of these goals, of course, depends upon the nation's continued commitment to religious freedom and tolerance—a commitment that posed a perennial challenge even before there was such a thing as an American nation. Indeed, the lofty standing of religious pluralism in America is not new. James Madison, one of the Founding Fathers of our democracy, emphasized that religious pluralism is not a threat to the stability of America, but rather, a positive force. He pointed out that the rights of individuals and those in the minority are better protected in a diverse society, since even those in the ruling majority must represent a wide variety of interests and perspectives.

Islam: A Mosaic, Not a Monolith began to take shape in the summer of 2001 as a brief report to the trustees of Carnegie Corporation. It was intended to provide historical context for possible grant-making initiatives in the future. But after the September 11, 2001, terrorist attacks, we decided that the report should have a global perspective and should not be confined to American Muslim communities. The "report" then grew into this more comprehensive survey that provides highlights from fourteen centuries of Islamic history.

Presenting such a wide-angle view in a relatively small space requires the free use of generalizations, summaries, and categorizations that must leave out many nuances of history. My intent is to simplify Islam without being simplistic, especially in describing the use and abuse of religion as a means to political ends—tribal, dynastic, economic, regional, and even international. I also aim to provide an American perspective on the challenges facing Muslim realms—a perspective that I think will interest Muslims at home as well as abroad. In writing for the general reader in the United States, I have used many readily available primary and secondary sources, including information from periodicals in English, while specifically avoiding Persian, Turkish, Arabic, and other sources that would not be easily accessible to them.

I have tried to be fair and judicious in discussing issues that are intensely controversial. I see this survey as exposition, not advocacy—with some exceptions. I do warn of some of the possible pitfalls of categorization. I do draw attention to the necessity for Americans to study religion's role in history and in contemporary society. I also encourage the promotion of understanding among cultures, civilizations, and religions, especially among the three Abrahamic faiths: Judaism, Christianity, and Islam. Religion, after all, has played a pivotal role in societies, and its study and understanding are necessary, not only in the West but also in the Muslim societies where there is a huge gap in understanding between leaders of secular thought and religious leaders.

The title of this survey offers a note of caution. As a historian, I have witnessed the nefarious consequences of categorization and the "aesthetization of politics," including ascribing sets of precise historical identities and attributes to entire communities, nations, and civilizations—and then judging the members of these groups based on such categorical imperatives, ignoring the differences, nuances, ambiguities, and "inconvenient" facts that tend to undermine neat theoretical frameworks.

During the past year, preceding and following the initial publication of this survey, we at Carnegie Corporation have begun to explore how we could assist those institutions and organizations that are committed to promoting American understanding of Islam as a religion, the characteristics of Muslim societies, in general, and those of American Muslim communities, in particular. We hope to examine ways to promote intergroup and interfaith understanding within our pluralistic democracy—and especially among the three Abrahamic faiths. We also hope to identify the best means to facilitate multilateral dialogues among Western and Muslim intellectuals, professionals, and clerics, as well as between Muslim secular intellectuals and theologians. In this connection, Carnegie Corporation, joined by the McArthur Foundation and the Rockefeller Brothers Foundation, sponsored the first international conference on Islam, in Spain in October 2002. We contemplate holding other conferences that may be sponsored in cooperation with our sister institutions in the United States and Europe and, whenever possible, with our counterparts in Africa, the Middle East, South Asia, and Southeast Asia.

These international dialogues and conferences, we hope, will produce a variety of critical, scholarly, and yet accessible texts on many of the issues raised in this survey. It is our ardent hope that such studies will, in turn, provide a common vocabulary and terms of reference for Muslims and non-Muslims alike, in the United States and abroad. We also hope that these efforts may provide a bridge of understanding between Americans and Muslim immigrants—as well as between Muslim Americans and their countries of origin. We are convinced that American Muslim communities are best equipped to help Muslim societies around the world better understand America, its institutions, democracy, pluralistic society, and traditions of religious tolerance.

We take heart in the strong public interest in this book and are gratified that, thanks to the Brookings Institution, it will now receive a wider audience.

I am indebted to members of Carnegie Corporation's Public Affairs Department: Susan King, Eleanor Lerman, Aimée Sisco, Ron Sexton, Grace Walters, Ambika Kapur, Maggie Vargas, Olga Fomitcheva; and my special thanks to Michael deCourcy Hinds.

 *Introduction*

$\mathcal{A}$LTHOUGH MORE THAN a year has passed since the attacks of September 11, 2001, most Americans still have such a sketchy knowledge of Islam that we probably need to keep ourselves focused on President George W. Bush's repeated reminders that terrorists, not Muslims or Arabs, are the enemy. That reasoned message, however, is often drowned out by noisy ones from some Muslim clerics, who call America the "Great Satan," and some political theorists, who interpret the war cries of militant Islamists as the start of a "clash of civilizations."[1] Provocative messages always gain a disproportionate amount of public attention, but they must be carefully considered and put in context.

It will surprise many Americans that Islam is the world's, and America's, fastest growing religion. It continues to grow at a rate faster than that of the world's population. If current trends continue, according to some estimates, it will have more adherents by the year 2023 than any other faith.

Most Americans tend to think of Islam as exclusively a religion of Arabs. But Muslims are as diverse as humanity itself, representing one in five people in the world. Only 15 percent of the world's 1.2 billion Muslims are Arabs, while nearly one in three Muslims lives on the Indian subcontinent. The largest Muslim nation is Indonesia, with 160 million Muslims among its 200 million people. Muslims represent the majority population in more than fifty nations, and they also constitute important minorities in many other countries. Muslims comprise at least 10 percent of the Russian Federation's population, 3 percent of China's population, and 3 to 4 percent of Europe's population. Islam is the second largest religion in France and the third largest in both Germany and Great Britain. Although estimates vary widely, Muslims represent 1 or 2 percent of the U.S. population, and some say there are more Muslims than Jews or Episcopalians in America. Religious, cultural, and population centers for Muslims, then, are no longer limited to such places as Mecca, Cairo, Baghdad, Teheran, Islamabad, Kuala Lumpur, Jakarta, Fez, and Damascus—they also include Paris, Berlin, London, and now New York, Detroit, Los Angeles, and Washington, D.C.[2]

Many Americans do not know that there are Christian Arabs as well as Muslim Arabs. Indeed, some of the oldest Christian churches—including the Coptic, Orthodox, Jacobite, and Maronite churches—rose, functioned, and still do, in Arab countries.

Given America's role as a magnet for immigrants, it is not surprising that the United States is one of the best reflections of Muslim diversity. "It is of the greatest interest and significance that the Muslim *umma*, or community, of North America is as nearly a microcosm of the global umma as has ever occurred since Islam became a major religion," writes Lawrence H. Mamiya.[3] American Muslims bring a rich ethnic heritage from South Asian countries (such as India, Bangladesh, Pakistan, Afghanistan), Southeast Asian countries (such as Malaysia, Indonesia, and the Philippines), all Arab nations, Iran, and Turkey. American Muslims also add their African, Caribbean, and European heritage to the nation's mix.[4]

With the United States currently the world's sole military and economic superpower, I believe that we, as a society, have a responsibility—for our own sake as well as for others'—to know the complex nature of the world, its incredibly rich variety of races, nations, tribes, languages, economies, cultures, and religions. Today, of course, Islam has become one of the major topics of discussion and controversy in the United States and elsewhere. Yet there is a disconnect between our passions about Islam and our knowledge of it.

It has become essential for us to understand Islam as a religion, its unity, diversity, and culture—and to appreciate the legacy of Islamic civilizations, their roles in the development of modern civilizations, the roles of Muslim nations and the challenges they face, and their future place in the world. This is much easier said than done, especially because in America today there is unfortunately no deep national commitment to history and heritage— not to our own, and certainly not to that of the world at large.

ONE

A Brief Survey
of Islam

To UNDERSTAND ISLAM, one has to appreciate the central role of Prophet Muhammad ibn Abdallah (570–632) in the formation and propagation of Islam as a religion. Muhammad was an Arab merchant, respected and wealthy, who belonged to the Qureish tribe in Mecca, then a great trading and religious center of polytheistic Arabia. His father had died before his birth, and his mother died in his early childhood. He was brought up by his grandfather and, after his death, by his uncle Abu Talib, whose son Ali ibn Abi Talib became the Prophet's first disciple and later his son-in-law.

Muslims believe that Muhammad, following God's instructions through the Archangel Gabriel, called humanity to a faith acknowledging *Allah*. Contrary to what many believe, Allah was not a new god, but simply the Arabic word for God—the God of Abraham, Moses, Jesus, and Muhammad. According to Muslim tradition, the Prophet Muhammad brought a message of continuity with Judaism and Christianity to the polytheistic tribes of Arabia. His message was an uncompromising, nonidolatrous monotheism. The faith was *Islam*, the Arabic verb meaning "surrender" or "submission," as in surrendering to God's will. *Muslim* is the active participle of the verb islam, meaning "I surrender." (Qur'an: "With God, the religion is Islam" and "It is a cult of your father, Abraham. He was the one who named you Muslims.")[1]

Islam, like Judaism and Christianity, is a prophetic religion. It, too, emphasizes God's relationship to humanity and reveals God's will through the medium of prophets—with warnings of punishment that will befall those who reject the divine message or are guilty of the cardinal sin of idolatry. (Qur'an: "Say ye: we believe in Allah, and the revelation given to us, and to Abraham, Ismail, Isaac, Jacob, and all the tribes. And, to that given to Moses and Jesus, and that given to [all] prophets from their Lord. We make no difference between one and another of them.")[2]

Muslims believe that the Prophet Muhammad received divine revelations from 610, starting in the ninth lunar month, *Ramadan*, until his death in 632, and that these oracles were transcribed during his lifetime and, within subsequent decades, were officially collected in the Qur'an, from the Arabic verb *qara'a*, meaning to recite, read, or transmit. The Qur'an, which Muslims consider to be a supernatural text, has 114 chapters (*suras*) of varying lengths, from 3 to 286 lines, which are arranged not in chronological or narrative order, but rather by their length, with the longest chapter near the beginning and the shortest chapter last.[3] Many non-Muslims might be surprised to see the numerous references to biblical stories and figures. Writing about the universality of the

Qur'an, the scholar Mohamed Talbi refers to a saying attributed to the Prophet Muhammad that the Qur'an is "God's Banquet," to which everyone is invited, but not obligated, to attend—people should come to him out of love, not compulsion.[4] Muslims consider the Qur'an to be the revealed and eternal Word of God and believe that it "completes and perfects" the revelations given to earlier prophets, including Moses and Jesus. They maintain that Muhammad was the greatest prophet and that he was the last one.

Muslims also believe that since God spoke to Muhammad through the Archangel Gabriel in Arabic, translations of the Qur'an are considered to be mere "interpretations." Even though the vast majority of Muslims do not understand Arabic, only the original Arabic is used in Muslim prayers, in the belief that the faithful can experience the presence of God by reading the Qur'an aloud. Some of the oldest surviving copies of the Qur'an apparently date from the start of the eighth century, but more than a thousand years passed before questions of spelling, the structure of the text, and rules for recitation were finally formalized with its publication in Cairo between 1919 and 1928.[5]

The fundamental principles of Islam are *Towhid*, unity of God; *Nowbowat*, belief in the prophetic mission of Muhammad; and *Ma'ad*, belief in the day of judgment and resurrection. In addition, Islam has five cardinal tenets, called the Pillars of Faith, that all Muslims must observe. They must

—bear witness, *Shihada*, that "there is no God but God, and Muhammad is his Prophet";

—pray five times a day, as a regular reminder of their commitment to Islam. To symbolize the unity of the faithful, the earliest Muslims oriented their prayers toward Jerusalem, and later on, toward Mecca. Muslims must prostrate themselves in prayer, repeatedly touching their foreheads to the ground, to dispel arrogance and promote humility;

—give a portion of their income as a tax, *zakat*, and one-fifth of their income, *khoums*, to the poor. The zakat, meaning "purification," and the gifts to the poor are based on the concept that a society cannot be pure as long as there is hunger and misery;

—fast during the day for the whole month of Ramadan, to experience hunger—that most visceral suffering of the poor;

—make at least one pilgrimage to Mecca, if physically and financially able.

In addition to the Qur'an and its Five Pillars, the study of Prophet Muhammad's life, known as the *sunna*, became a part of the Islamic faith, law, and theology. This occurred because Muhammad was considered to be the Perfect Man, and though he was not deemed divine, his life eventually became a source of inspiration and a guide to practicing Muslims. "By imitating the smallest details of his external life and by reproducing the way he ate, washed, loved, spoke, and prayed, Muslims hoped to be able to acquire his interior attitude of perfect surrender to God," writes Karen Armstrong.[6]

The sunna, the oral history of the Prophet, is the second most important source of Islamic law, after the Qur'an. The third source is the *hadith*, which consists of thousands of references to Prophet Muhammad's sayings and teachings that are documented through a meticulously reconstructed, uninterrupted chain of people, traced to his immediate family and entourage. The entire body of Islamic law is called the *Sharia*, or "straight path to God."

The Sharia has five main sources: the Qur'an, the sunna, the hadith, legal analogies based on the Qur'an and the hadith, and legal decisions that arise from consensus, in the belief that God would not allow the whole community to go astray.[7] (Some strict schools of Islamic law do not accord the latter two sources, or even the hadith, much weight, and in addition, Muslim denominations differ on whether the Sharia is still evolving or is a closed book.)

The Qur'an singles out Jews and Christians as "People of the Book" and sets them apart from nonbelievers. After all, Jews and Christians, like Muslims, worshiped the transcendent God of Abraham. But the book mentioned is not the Bible; it refers to a heavenly text, written by God, of which the Qur'an, according to Muslims, is the only perfect manifestation.[8]

As in Judaism and Christianity, Abraham, *Ibrahim*, occupies a central place in Islam. Abraham is at the root of all three religions: just as Jews trace their lineage to Abraham and his wife, Sarah, through their son, Isaac, the Arabs trace their genealogy to Abraham and Hagar—Sarah's Egyptian maid—through their son, Ishmael, *Ismail*.[9] In the Qur'an, Abraham is recognized as the first Muslim because he surrendered to God rather than accept the idolatrous religion of his parents. There are more than sixty references to Abraham in the Qur'an, and he is called *Hanif*, a "True Monotheist"; *Khalil*, a "Friend of God"; and even Umma, "Muslim community," for initially he was the entire faith community. In every Muslim prayer, Ibrahim is mentioned.[10] Muslims believe that it was Abraham and Ishmael who rebuilt Islam's holiest shrine in Mecca—the *Kaaba*, believed to be the oldest monotheistic temple, which some Muslim traditions trace to Adam. The cube-shaped Kaaba is made of stone and marble, and its interior contains pillars and silver and gold lamps; it is entered only twice a year, for a ritual cleansing ceremony.[11]

Moses is also considered to be a great prophet. His confrontation with the Egyptian pharaoh, his miracles in the desert, and his ascent of the mountain to receive God's commandments are all acknowledged in the Qur'an.[12]

For Muslims, Jesus, *Isa*, is a great prophet and messenger of God—the promised Messiah who brought "the Word of God and Spirit from Him." Jesus is considered the son of the "sinless" Virgin Mary, *Maryam*, who is mentioned more often in the Qur'an than in the Bible.[13] Muslims believe that Jesus preached the Word of God and worked miracles; but like Jews, Muslims reject the Christian concept of Jesus as the divine son of God. Muslims consider that blasphemy, for they believe there is only one divinity, God. The crucifixion of Christ is mentioned in passing only, and the Qur'an states that Jesus did not die, but was rescued by God and taken to heaven.[14] In the end, Jesus and the other prophets will descend to be at the final judgment. Muslims also believe that Jesus' true message had been misinterpreted by his followers and that the Prophet Muhammad was sent to bring the definitive message of God.[15]

Of course, there are many important similarities and differences among the religions. To mention just a few more: Jews do not accept the New Testament, but Muslims do. The miracles of Jesus, his virgin birth, and his second coming are accepted in Islam, but not in Judaism. Both Judaism and Islam put great importance on living according to a system of law—for Jews, the law is the Halakhah; for Muslims it is the Sharia.[16] In Christianity, which has the concept of original sin, humans are born as sinners; but in both Judaism and Islam, sin is not present at birth and accrues only through sinful activity. Both Judaism and Islam share similar dietary restrictions, including bans on eating pork or blood, though the Islamic rules are generally less restrictive than Judaism's.[17] And, as are Christian and Jewish children, Muslim children are freely given biblical names: Solomons and Sulaimans, Sarahs and Sirahs, Josephs and Yusufs, Marys and Maryams, Jesuses and Isas, Johns and Yahyas, and Davids and Davuds, to cite a few.

The Phenomenal Spread of Islam

In 622, having challenged the polytheist practices in Mecca, Muhammad fled for safety to Yatrib, subsequently named Medina, the City of the Prophet. This event, called the *Hijra*, marks the start of the Islamic era and of the Islamic calendar.

The early spread of Islam is one of the most dramatic chapters in all history. By 632, when Islam was only a decade old and just solidifying into a religion, almost all the tribes of Arabia had converted to Islam or joined Prophet Muhammad's confederacy. Within less than a century of Islam's birth, the Muslim community had grown by conquest into one of the largest empires ever— one that lasted longer and, indeed, was bigger than the Roman Empire.[18] By 712, Muslim conquests extended from the Pyrenees to the Himalayas, from the Iberian Peninsula in the west to the Indus Valley and Central Asia in the east. Muslims advanced into Europe until stopped in what is now western France in 732 by Charles Martel, king of the Franks, at the Battle of Poitiers.[19]

The Muslim Calendar

Year 1 on the Muslim calendar starts with the Hijra, which is assumed to have taken place on July 16, 622, in the Julian calendar (which predates the Gregorian calendar, now used almost universally). Thus 2003 A.D. is 1423 A.H., or Anno Hegirae, the year of the Hijra. Although 1,381 years (2003 minus 622) have passed in the Gregorian calendar, 1,423 years have passed in the Islamic lunar calendar, because its year is consistently shorter (by about eleven days). The Islamic calendar is used primarily for religious purposes and cannot be accurately printed in advance because it is based on human sightings of the lunar crescent, which vary depending on the observer's location, atmospheric conditions, and local weather. Some countries, including Saudi Arabia, do use the Islamic calendar in daily life but calculate the calendar in advance by using astronomical data rather than visual sightings of the moon.[1]

1. For history and conversion of dates, see Tarek's Hijri/Gregorian/Julian Converter (http://bennyhills.fortunecity.com/elfman/454/calindex.html# TOP).

Historians point out that Islam arose at the right time and place. In the sixth and early seventh centuries, a power vacuum emerged after protracted wars between the Persian and Byzantine empires had weakened both. As Muslims conquered Palestine, Syria, Egypt, and Armenia, they promoted conversion to Islam in several ways. They gave polytheists the option of conversion or death (Qur'an: "Slay the polytheists wherever you find them. But if they repent, and perform the prayer, and pay the alms, then let them go their way; God is all-forgiving, all-compassionate").[20] Jews and Christians were not required to become Muslims; however, if they did not convert they were tolerated as subjects but not given equality, and they were required to pay a burdensome tax, *jizya*, ostensibly to pay for Muslim protection. There were also voluntary conversions, not only for religious reasons, but also for the practical reasons of securing social and economic advantages in an Islamic society. For many converts, Islam might have had a comforting familiarity, embracing as it did monotheism and biblical messages that Judaism and Christianity had spread for many centuries before Muhammad began preaching around 610. St. John of Damascus, who chronicled Islam in the eighth century, regarded Islam not as a new religion, but as a branch of Christianity.[21]

Historians emphasize that Islam also spread rapidly because of its extraordinary acceptance of diversity from the beginning—reminding us that Islam grew organically and not as an inflexible religion. We know that in some conquered lands of the Byzantine empire, the inhabitants had been persecuted, sometimes oppressed and heavily taxed by Christian rulers, and some minorities naturally welcomed the new Muslim rulers with their relatively tolerant religious policies. Islam also appeared to be far more accommodating than Christianity to other cultures—so accommodating, in fact, that apart from the Five Pillars, the practice of Islam varied enormously from place to place and often included practices and beliefs that were not consistent with the Qur'an.[22] The rich legacy of Islamic civilizations, historians argue, is due in part to its exceptional absorptive quality and relative tolerance for different cultures and ethnic traditions of civilizations from southern Europe to Central Asia and the Indian subcontinent.

Early Divisions in Islam

Unlike Christians, who consider the whole Church to be the mystical body of Christ, Islam did not sustain a centralized organization. Instead, Prophet Muhammad's *khulafah*, Caliphs or successors, provided leadership, but succession disputes frequently arose and divided—and redivided—the faithful. Religious authority became increasingly dispersed among the *ulama*, scholars and clerics, in numerous Islamic denominations spread throughout Muslim realms.

The debate over succession began immediately after Prophet Muhammad's death, for he had left no indisputable instructions about the rules of succession or whether spiritual leaders were also political leaders. Since Muhammad did not have a son, one faction wanted the Caliph to be elected from the ranks of respected leaders in the umma, the Muslim community. A rival group contended that the leadership should be confined to the Prophet's immediate family and descendants. His closest surviving male relative was Ali ibn Abi Talib, who was both a cousin and the husband of his daughter Fatima, as well as the father of two of Muhammad's grandchildren, Hasan and Husayn.[23]

We know from history that, in this instance, election won out over heredity. But before the century was over, much Muslim blood was to be spilled in civil wars tied to the widening rifts over succession and legitimacy. Muhammad's first successor was Abu Bakr, a compromise candidate because he was an honored leader as well as one of Muhammad's fathers-in-law. Abu Bakr was the first of the four "Rightly Guided Caliphs," as the first leaders are known. All four had been close companions of the Prophet and were considered authoritative sources of information about the Prophet's life and teachings.[24] Abu Bakr died a natural death, but the next three Rightly Guided Caliphs were all assassinated: Umar ibn al-Khattab in 644; Uthman ibn Affan in 656; and Ali ibn Abi Talib, Muhammad's son-in-law, in 661. These assassinations sparked violent conflicts or outright wars.

Indeed, the theological and political consequences of these struggles over succession were far reaching. After Ali's assassination, *Shiat Ali*, the Party of Ali, created its own Shii branch of Islam. Initially, the break was over the succession dispute, with the Shii favoring a succession based on blood ties to the Prophet. Muslims who favored an elective system came to be known as *Sunni*, taking their name from sunna, which in this context refers to the customs, actions, and sayings attributed to the Prophet and the first four Caliphs.[25] (Otherwise, sunna refers only to the Prophet's sayings and deeds.)[26] Early divisions in Islam ultimately resulted in scores of Muslim denominations.[27]

But calling this break a dispute over succession does not nearly tell the whole story. In his recent book, Khalid Durán notes, "The conflict between Sunnism and Shi'ism resembles that between Judaism and Christianity. Just as Christians have held Jews responsible for the killing of Christ, Shi'is hold Sunnis responsible for the killing of 'Alî and his sons, Hasan and [Husayn]." '*Âshûrâ*', for example, is a religious holiday for both Shii and Sunni, but while the Shii mourn the anniversary of Husayn's assassination, the Sunni have joyful celebrations commemorating God's mercy in delivering the Israelites from Egyptian bondage—Passover, in Judaism.[28]

Islam also developed a mystical component, Sufism, that drew followers—as well as fierce and sometimes violent adversaries—from both Shii and Sunni Muslims. Sufism is named after the coarse shirts of wool, *souf*, worn by early ascetics, who were reformers and, according to some mainstream Muslims, heretics.[29]

Even thumbnail sketches of each of the three main Muslim denominations convey a sense of Islam's complexity as a religion.

SUNNI

The Sunni represent the overwhelming majority of Muslims, but Sunni doctrine has long been a source of dispute. In the eighth and ninth centuries, there was a major theological conflict among the Sunni that has echoed throughout Islamic history. On one side, some schools of theology were led by *Mu'tazilite* scholars in Basra and Baghdad. They used rational proofs for God and the universe, as they sought to harmonize reason with Muslim scriptures, proclaiming—blasphemously, to some—that the Qur'an was man-made and was not the eternal truth revealed by God. The Mu'tazilite scholars called for a rational theology, arguing that God has a rational nature and that moral laws and free will were part of the unchangeable essence of reason. The movement was the result of the encounter of Islam with earlier civilizations—Persian and Greco-Roman—and especially with the traditions of Greek philosophy.

A few early Caliphs tried to enforce this rational approach as the exclusive interpretation of Islam. Had they been successful, they would have solidified their authority not only as political leaders but also as the final arbiters of religious law. But in 848, after Mu'tazilism had been the Caliphate's official doctrine for several decades, Caliph al-Mutawakkil succumbed to widespread opposition from the ulama, the religious establishment. As the Caliphate saw its religious authority chipped away, the Caliphs' claim to rule as successors of the Prophet came under increasing attack from the ulama. The resulting loss of a central religious authority meant that, for Sunni Muslims, there would be many interpreters within the ulama at many theological centers in many regions.

SHII

Shii believe that Ali, the Prophet's son-in-law, was divinely inspired and infallible in his interpretations of the Qur'an and the Prophet's teachings and that only his descendants possessed the sacred blood ties and religious knowledge to qualify as *Imams*, the Shii's exemplary leaders.

Hence, according to Shii theology, called *Imami*, the line of succession passed through Ali and Fatima, and the Imam could be any male descendant of their sons, Hasan and Husayn. Difficulties arose after Ali and Fatima's elder son, Hasan, died in 669, and their second son, Husayn, along with relatives and friends, was assassinated in 680 in the Battle of Karbala, after challenging the authority of the ruling Caliph Yazid ibn Muawiyyah and asserting his right to the Prophet's succession. Ali's third son (with another wife), Hanafiyya, died in 700. Shii sects developed around each

The Origins of the Qur'an

There is relatively little contemporary research about the origins of the Qur'an, and to some degree, research efforts have been dampened by both "political correctness" and fear of retribution—such as Ayatullah Khomeini's 1989 *fatwa* (decree) condemning Salman Rushdie to death for writing *The Satanic Verses*. But a number of scholars have taken a revisionist look at Islamic history.[1] Patricia Crone, a professor in the School of Historical Studies at the Institute for Advanced Studies at Princeton, says it is paradoxical that Muhammad, whom many believe to have been an illiterate merchant in a remote and pagan land, would have known so much about Abraham, Moses, and other prophets—unless one believes, as faithful Muslims do, that the Archangel Gabriel revealed this history to Muhammad.

Martin Bright, summarizing revisionist trends in scholarship on Islamic history, suggests "that we know almost nothing about the life of Prophet Mohammad; that the rapid rise of the religion can be attributed, at least in part, to the attraction of Islam's message of conquest and jihad for the tribes of the Arabian peninsula; that the [Qur'an] as we know it today was compiled, or perhaps even written, long after Mohammad's supposed death in 632 A.D. Most controversially of all, the researchers say that there existed an anti-Christian alliance between Arabs and Jews in the earliest days of Islam, and that the religion may be best understood as a heretical branch of rabbinical Judaism." In a terse rebuttal, Ziauddin Sardar, a Muslim intellectual, called this "Eurocentrism of the most extreme, purblind kind, which assumes that not a single word written by Muslims can be accepted as evidence." Suggesting that the Qur'an had human authors is, of course, as blasphemous to Muslims as the Qur'an's denial of Jesus' divinity is to Christians.[2]

A new scholarly work, written under the pseudonym Christopher Luxenberg and published in Berlin, argues that the Qur'an is based on earlier Christian Aramaic manuscripts, which were later misinterpreted by Islamic scholars. Luxenberg notes that the original text of the Qur'an was written without vowels or accent marks, requiring Islamic scholars in the eighth and ninth centuries to make clarifications—and allowing errors to be introduced. For example, he asserts that Aramaic descriptions of paradise, which seem to be echoed in the Qur'an, portray paradise as a lush garden with pooling water and trees with rare fruit, including white raisins—raisins, *not* virgin maidens, as promised in the Qur'an and nowadays allegedly offered as a lure by militant Islamists to suicide bombers in Palestine. Other historians note that there is no sign of the Qur'an until 691, or fifty-nine years after Muhammad's death.[3]

Many Muslim scholars have rejected this revisionist scholarship.[4]

1. See Patricia Crone and Michael Cook, *Hagarism: The Making of the Islamic World* (Cambridge University Press, 1977); Patricia Crone, *Meccan Trade and the Rise of Islam* (Princeton University Press, 1987); and Patricia Crone, "The Rise of Islam in the World," in Francis Robinson, ed., *The Cambridge Illustrated History of the Islamic World* (Cambridge University Press, 1999).

2. Martin Bright, "The Great Koran Con-Trick," *New Statesman*, December 10, 2001, pp. 25–27. Sardar's rebuttal appears in the same issue.

3. See Alexander Stille, "Scholars Are Quietly Offering New Theories of the Koran," *New York Times*, March 2, 2002, p. A1.

4. For a Muslim response to questions of the Qur'an's authenticity, see Abdur-Raheem Green, "Uncomfortable Questions: An Authoritative Exposition," *Muslim Answers* (www.muslim-answers.org/expo-01.htm, www.muslim-answers.org/expo-02.htm).

son, the *Hanafids*, the *Husaynids*, and the *Hasanids*. Other denominations also emerged around other branches of the Prophet's clan.

Succession disputes were intensified when there was more than one male descendant; in one instance, Muhammad al-Baqir, the fifth Imam, denied his brother's claim to be Imam by asserting that he, like prior Imams, had a mystical ability to interpret the Qur'an and had also been anointed by his father. His brother, Zayd ibn Ali, challenged that view and developed his own following.[30] The *Zaydis* are one of three major Shii sects:

Zaydis. This sect believed that the Imam could be any male descendant of Ali and Fatima's sons, Hasan and Husayn. The Imam was also expected to be a learned man, namely an expert in Islamic law, as well as an able warrior. But unlike some other sects, its followers did not believe the Imam was infallible. More than one Imam could be present, in different territories, and an Imam could be deposed if deemed sinful. During times when there was no Imam—as is the case today in Yemen, where most Zaydis live—spiritual leadership was vested in Zaydi scholars until a new Imam arrived.

Ismailis. In the eighth century, there was a Shii conflict over which son of Imam Ja'far al-Sadiq should succeed him: Ismail ibn Ja'far or his younger brother, Musa al-Kazim. Each brother developed his own following. Ismail's followers—Ismailis—revere him as the last of Ali and Fatima's descendants. The Ismailis, unlike the Zaydis, consider the Imam infallible. Another major succession dispute, also between two brothers, arose in the eleventh century and split the Ismailis into two major denominations—one led today by the Aga Khan and another known as the Buhura Ismailis.[31] Many smaller Ismaili sects appeared as well.[32]

Twelvers. While the Ismailis followed Ismail ibn Ja'far and his descendants, the Twelver Shii followed the lineage of his brother, Musa al-Kazim. This group had many conflicts with Sunni Muslims, who kept several of their Imams under house arrest. Many Imams were apparently poisoned as well, including the eleventh Imam. The twelfth Imam, a young boy, disappeared in 874. His followers—who, in his honor, adopted the name Twelvers— believe that God rescued him, that he was "occluded" (taken up), and that he will return as a messiah to restore peace and justice in the world. Until he returns, political and religious authority are exercised, fallibly, by the clergy; in order of rising rank, these include *mujtahids, hujjatu-l-islam, ayatullah, ayatullah 'uzma,* and, the highest rank, *marja'-e-taqlîd,* the one who sets the norms to be followed. Ayatullah, meaning "sign of God," is used only among Shii in Iran; it first appeared in the eighteenth century, invented by a king who, like monarchs everywhere then, coined and sold titles, including this one.[33] (Ayatullah 'Uzma Ruhollah Khomeini, who led the 1979 revolution in Iran, was often called "Imam." This was an innovation because, unlike in Sunni Islam, in Twelver Shii Islam the term *Imam* refers only to the twelve Imams. Ayatullah Khomeini stressed the point that he was imam only in the sense of prayer leader and spiritual guide and nothing more.)[34]

The Shii, and especially the Twelvers, have developed a vast and complex religious hierarchy that may be comparable, in some ways, to the structure of Christian churches. In this regard, the

Shii are also very different from the Sunni, who, somewhat inconsistently, have many religious leaders but no religious hierarchy of
such complexity; they consider Islam to be a decentralized religion.[35] Indeed, it is this decentralization that gives rise to persist-
ent questions about who has authority to speak for Islam.

Twelvers believed that religious principles could be found
through use of God-given reason, though these principles could
not contradict the Qur'an or the sayings of the Prophet or the
twelve Imams—for these sacred texts were believed to contain all
the rules of reason. The Twelver school of law was developed by
Imam Ja'far al-Sadiq, the sixth Imam—hence its name, *Ja'fari*.
The Ja'fari accorded equal weight to the behavior and sayings of
the infallible Imams and to those of the Prophet. In addition,
other ulama advocated various levels of independent reason as
acceptable in applying the hadith and Qur'an to issues of the day.
On one side, the *Usulis* felt free to use analogies and rationality in
interpreting the sacred texts; at the other end of the spectrum, the
Akhbaris insisted on a strict, literal reading. The Twelver denomination has about 140 million members in more than a dozen
nations today. Twelver Shiism became the official religion of
Iranians during the Safavid empire in the early sixteenth century.
Currently, there are also Twelvers in Pakistan, Iraq, Saudi Arabia,
Bahrain, and other countries.[36]

SUFI

Within Islam's many denominations, Sufism developed in the
tenth century as an early effort to reform Islam, in part by empha-
sizing spiritual rewards in the afterlife rather than material gains
in this life, and in part by challenging literal, legalistic approaches

to Islam and the Qur'an. Sufis seek to commune directly with God through meditation, ritual chanting, and even dance (the *Mevlavi* Sufis were famously known as the whirling dervishes). Some Sufis even worshiped Jesus and others worshiped Muhammad—practices considered polytheistic and blasphemous to mainstream Muslims, who sometimes persecuted the Sufis.[37] Yet Sufis often served as Islam's most energetic missionaries, in addition to their many contributions to Muslim literature, especially love poetry, in Arabic, Turkish, Persian and Urdu.[38] Sufism has been called Islam's "counterculture."[39]

This cursory description of Islam's denominations illustrates the wide and deep theological divisions within what might appear from the outside to be a monolithic religion. These divisions, in turn, led to extremely complex and varied theological and political differences, even within mainstream Sunni Islam.

PREVENTING NEW INTERPRETATIONS OF THE QUR'AN AND HADITH

The efforts of the ulama to formalize Islamic doctrine for mainstream Sunni Muslims led to the emergence of four prominent schools of Islamic law in the eighth and ninth centuries. They made a religious science out of hadith by checking the authenticity of each link in the chain of sources of oral history and resolving discrepancies in reports on the Prophet's words and deeds. These schools, still influential today, are the *Hanafi*—named after Abu Hanifah—which is now followed in parts of South Asia, Turkey, the Russian Federation (with the exception of the North Caucasus), southeastern Europe, China, Central and West Asia,

Authenticating the Tradition

Researching the chain of sources is a daunting task, as suggested by the following hadith, a narrative about sins that was passed down through half a dozen people: "Hisham ibn 'Ummar said that Sadaqa ibn Khalid told him that 'Abd al-Rahman ibn Yazid told him that 'Atiya ibn Qays al-Kilabi told him that 'Abd al-Rahman ibn Ghanm al-Ash'ari told him that Abu 'Amir or Abu Malik al-Ash'ari who, by God, did not lie to him, said that he heard the Prophet saying: 'Among my people, there will be some who will consider illicit sex, wearing silk, drinking wine, and playing musical instruments as permitted. There will also be some people who will dwell near the side of a hill. Someone will deliver their roving animals to them, coming to them out of a need. They will say to him to come back tomorrow. God will plot against them at night and will let the hill crush them and He will change the rest of them into monkeys and pigs leaving them like that until the day of resurrection.'"[1]

1. Andrew Rippin and Jan Knappert, eds. and trans., *Textual Sources for the Study of Islam* (Chicago: University of Chicago Press, 1990), p. 74.

and parts of the Middle East; *Maliki*—named after Malik ibn Anas—which is followed in North and West Africa and in some southern parts of the Middle East; *Shafi*—named after Muhammad ibn Idris al-Shafi—which is followed in the coastal areas of South Asia and in East Africa, East Asia, Egypt, and some parts of the Middle East; and *Hanbali*—named after Ahmad ibn Hanbal—which is followed mostly in Saudi Arabia.

The schools varied in the amount of leeway they allowed in interpreting Sharia (Islamic law) and whether they believed those interpretations could be made by individual scholars or had to be endorsed by a consensus of scholars.[40] The Malikis and the Hanbalis read the scripture and hadith quite literally, scorning the use of human reason as it was employed by the other two, more interpretative schools. The Hanafis used analogy and reason, especially in untangling conflicting statements attributed to the Prophet. The Shafis sought to concentrate on the most authentic oral reports and looked to find a consensus among scholars on interpretive rulings.[41] The issue was—and still is—extremely important, because such interpretations became part of the Sharia, which Muslims consider to be the divinely revealed law of Islam.

In the tenth century, orthodox Sunni ulama argued that there had been enough of this independent reasoning and warned that it could not continue without distorting Islam. They maintained that the Sharia was completely and finally assembled within three centuries of Muhammad's death and it was time to "close the gates of ijtihad," or rational interpretation. This argument gained ground and was finally formalized in the fourteenth century, when Sunni ulama agreed that contemporary questions could be answered only by a literal reading of the Sharia and not by new interpretation.[42]

But many Muslim reformers, from the eleventh century on, objected to such a "mechanistic," literal approach to scripture and argued that the schools of law were too rigid in defining Sharia. Much debate has centered around the hadith, with reformers questioning the vast number of oral histories, the often conflicting interpretations of the hadith, and the ulama's ability to verify the Prophet's sayings as they were passed down through the ages by his friends, his family, and community members. Reformers in the past, and especially in the nineteenth century, attempted to portray the hadith as parables, not to be construed as religious doctrine or law—and certainly not to be used to diminish the exercise of God-given reason in addressing contemporary challenges. Different approaches to Sharia not only divided Sunni, but also sharpened the divisions and struggles between Sunni and Shii, because the Sunni believe the Sharia is complete, while the Shii consider it evolving jurisprudence.[43]

The Golden Age of Islam

The early, formative period of the Muslim empire was followed by the Abbasid Caliphate (750–1258), named after Caliph Abu al-Abbas al-Saffah, who claimed descent from an uncle of Muhammad's.[44] He transferred the seat of power from Damascus to Baghdad and inaugurated what is known as the Golden Age of Islamic civilization. This Golden Age is no mere footnote in Islamic history, for arguably "Islamic" civilization was essentially human civilization—one that, like prior Greek and Roman civilizations, embraced and thrived on all human achievement. As such, we are just beginning to recognize the enormous influence that Islam's Golden Age had on Western Christendom. As W. Montgomery Watt reminds us:

> It is clear that the influence of Islam on Western Christendom
> is greater than is usually realized. Not only did Islam share with

Western Europe many material products and technological dis-
coveries; not only did it stimulate Europe intellectually in the
fields of science and philosophy; but it provoked Europe into
forming a new image of itself. Because Europe was reacting
against Islam, it belittled the influence [of Muslim scholar-
ship]. . . . So today, an important task for our Western Europeans, as we move into the era of the one world, is to correct
this false emphasis and to acknowledge fully our debt to the
Arab and Islamic world.[45]

During those five "golden" centuries, Muslim realms became
the world's unrivaled intellectual centers of science, medicine,
philosophy, and education. The Abbasids championed the role of
knowledge and are renowned for such enlightened achievements
as creating a "House of Wisdom" in Baghdad, the city they built
on the banks of the Tigris river. At this Abbasid institute, Muslim
and non-Muslim scholars—including Nestorian Christians and
star-worshiping Sabians—sought to bring all the world's written
knowledge into Arabic.[46] Classic works by Aristotle, Archimedes,
Euclid, Hypocrites, Plutarch, Ptolemy, and others were translated.
Christian monks created Arabic versions of the Bible, and many
Jewish philosophers wrote in Arabic. Without these Arabic translations, it is interesting to note, many classic works of antiquity
would have been lost.

Furthermore, from the eleventh to the thirteenth centuries,
many Arabic translations of classic works were, in turn, translated
into Turkish, Persian, Hebrew, and Latin. Thus the thirteenth-
century Catholic theologian St. Thomas Aquinas apparently made
his famous integration of faith and reason after reading Aristotle's

philosophy in a translation by Abbasid scholars, including Abu Ali ibn Sina, known in the West as Avicenna.[47] Avicenna was an eleventh-century philosopher and physician who wrote an encyclopedia of philosophy and some 200 influential treatises on medicine, including one on ethics, which were widely read in Europe. The twelfth-century philosopher Abu al-Walid Muhammad ibn Ahmad ibn Muhammad ibn Rushd, better known in the West as Averroës, a preeminent authority on Aristotle, as well as a judge and a physician, is also known for having synthesized Greek and Arabic philosophies. Meanwhile, al-Farabi tried to show that the ideal political system envisaged in Plato's utopia and in the divine law of Islam were one and the same.

Not merely translators, the Abbasids collected, synthesized, and advanced knowledge, building their own civilization from intellectual gifts from many cultures, including Chinese, Indian, Iranian, Egyptian, North African, Greek, Spanish, Sicilian, and Byzantine. This period in Islam was indeed a cauldron of cultures, religions, learning, and knowledge—one that created great civilizations and influenced others from Africa to China. The Muslim Golden Age has been hailed for its open embrace of a universal science. There was just one science—not a separate "Christian science," "Jewish science," "Muslim science," "Zoroastrian science," or "Hindu science"—for the Abbasids, who were apparently influenced by numerous Qur'anic references to honoring God by learning about the wonders of the universe. Thus, reason and faith, both being God-given, were combined, mutually inclusive, and supportive; Islam was anything but isolationist. Non-Muslims—as well as today's doctrinaire Muslims who preach against "Western" values and "Western" science—may be shocked by the Abbasids' receptiveness to science and philosophies that challenged orthodoxy.

According to Ismail Serageldin,

> The search for Knowledge ('Ilm) and Truth (Haq) are an integral and undeniable part of the Muslim tradition. The pursuit of knowledge is the single most striking feature in a system of great revelation such as Islam. The word 'Ilm (knowledge) and its derivatives occur 880 times in the [Qur'an]. But knowledge is not perceived as neutral. It is the basis for better appreciating truth (Haq), which is revealed but which can be "seen" by the knowledgeable in the world around them. Indeed, believers are enjoined to look around and to learn the truth. The Prophet exhorted his followers to seek knowledge as far as China, then considered to be the end of the earth. Scientists are held in high esteem: the Prophet said that the ink of scientists is equal to the blood of martyrs.[48]

The Abbasids were not alone in the Islamic pursuit of knowledge. Rival Muslim dynasties—the Fatimids in Egypt and Umayyads in al-Andalus, or Islamic Spain—were also intellectual and cultural centers during parts of this period.[49] Al-Andalus, captured from its Gothic rulers, became part of the Islamic empire in 714 and rivaled Baghdad and Cairo in scholarship. Córdoba, its capital, is believed to have had seventy libraries, including one in the Alcázar with 400,000 volumes. Religious freedom, although limited, helped attract Jewish and Christian intellectuals and spawned the greatest period of creativity in philosophy during the Middle Ages as networks of Muslim, Jewish, and Christian philosophers interacted in the eleventh and twelfth centuries.[50]

Andalus was a great literary center, and its poetry about courtly, chaste, and chivalrous relationships has even been credited with helping shape European ideas about romantic love.[51]

Together, Abbasid, Fatimid, and Umayyad scholars opened up new fields of study and significantly advanced contemporary knowledge of astronomy, architecture, art, botany, ethics, geography, history, literature, mathematics, music, mechanics, medicine, mineralogy, philosophy, physics, and even veterinary medicine and zoology. During the Abbasid period, mathematicians pioneered integral calculus and spherical trigonometry, promoted the use of the "Arabic numerals," 0 through 9, and gave the world *al-jabr*, our algebra. In science, the Abbasids revised Ptolemaic astronomy, named stars, developed *al-kemia*, our chemistry, and demonstrated that science was, well, a science. Some may also thank, or damn, Abbasids for *al-kuhl*, our alcohol, which they learned to distill but were subsequently forbidden to drink.

Education was a high priority in Muslim empires during this period. By the tenth century, there were thousands of schools at *mosques*, places for kneeling, including 300 in Baghdad alone. A number of libraries gathered manuscripts from around the world, and schools that would become universities were established. Under the Fatimids, a mosque that opened for prayers in Cairo in 972 eventually grew into the University of Al-Azhar, the oldest university in the Mediterranean.[52]

Even during this Golden Age, Islam's civilization embraced multiple centers, making the civilization anything but a monolithic entity. Great Muslim learning centers were not confined to Medina, Basra, Kufa, and Damascus. Indeed, while Baghdad remained the cultural capital of Islamic realms from the eleventh to the middle of the thirteenth century, the proliferation of cultural and intellectual centers was evident in such cities as Jerusalem, Cairo, Kairouan, Fez, Córdoba, Toledo, and Seville—as well as many others in Iran, Afghanistan, and Central Asia, including Nishapur, Merv, Bukhara, Samarkand, Balkh, Herat, Ghazna, Rayy, Shiraz, Hamadan, and Isfahan.

FRAGMENTATION OF POLITICAL POWER

But even in Islam's Golden Age, political power was fragmented: not one, but three Caliphates—Abbasids, Fatimids, and Umayyads—ruled Muslim societies.

In 909, Shii Muslims of the Ismaili denomination established a Caliphate-Imam in Tunisia under leaders who claimed descent from the Prophet's son-in-law, Ali, and his daughter, Fatima—hence their name, Fatimids. The Fatimids captured Egypt in 969 and established their capital, al-Qahira—the "Victorious City"—Cairo.[53] The dynasty's rule at one time extended to the Mediterranean, North Africa, Syria, Iran, and India, and it lasted until 1171, when the last Fatimid Caliph was deposed.[54] It was Salah al-Din Yusuf ibn Ayyub, a Kurdish general known in the West as Saladin, who defeated the Fatimids in Egypt and brought the region's population back into the fold of Sunni Islam. Later, Saladin gained fame for defeating the Crusaders and recapturing Jerusalem in 1187. Saladin's Ayyubid dynasty (1171–1250) ruled over Egypt, Syria, and Yemen until members of its army, predominantly slaves called *Mamluks*, revolted and created their own empire in the Near East.[55]

In 929, twenty years after the Fatimid Caliph-Imam was established, another Caliphate sprang up. Abd al-Rahman III, who traced his ancestry to the Umayyad Caliphate, which the Abbasids had overthrown, proclaimed himself Caliph in al-Andalus. He assumed the title "Commander of the Faithful" and asserted independence from the Abbasid Caliphate in Baghdad and the newly independent Fatimid Caliph. He and his descendants ruled as Caliphs in Córdoba until 1031, when the Umayyad Caliphate was officially abolished as the central government collapsed amid infighting among regional leaders.[56]

In addition to Caliphates, other regional dynasties—kingdoms unto themselves—rose, fell, and reconstituted themselves again and again over the centuries. Notable among them in the early centuries of Islam were various Iranian and Turkic dynasties, including the *Samanids* and the *Shii Buyids*. The latter conquered Baghdad but maintained the Abbasid Caliphate.[57]

WEST AND EAST CLASH OVER TERRITORY

Much has been made of the early encounters between Muslim armies and the Crusaders and the impact on these wars on the course of history in the Middle East and subsequent relations between Christians and Muslims. The facts, however, do not fit easily into ideological patterns. We know that the Seljuq Turks invaded the Christian empire of Byzantium, setting off a chain of events that led to the Crusades—which history shows were mostly territorial wars often camouflaged in religious garb and language and carried out under the symbol of the cross. Initially, the Byzantine emperor sought help in fighting off the Seljuq Turks from Pope Urban II, who in turn wanted to strengthen his moral and political authority by capturing Jerusalem. Muslims had conquered the city in 638, and though they were generally tolerant of non-Muslims, Caliph-Imam al-Hakim bi-Amr Allah had ordered the destruction of the Church of the Holy Sepulchre in Jerusalem and other churches and convents in Egypt and Sinai during his twenty-five-year reign, which ended in 1021.[58]

In launching the "holy war" against Muslims, the Pope declared, "God wills it!" The Church promised Christian soldiers fighting in this war that, win or lose, they would have all their sins forgiven and a welcome in heaven—the kind of blanket guarantees that encouraged, and continue to encourage, "holy warriors" of every religion to commit crimes and atrocities. At the time, the Crusaders were known by the Muslims as Franks: members of a western Christian empire that included present-day France. They led their armies into what would later be called the First Crusade, capturing Jerusalem in 1099 and massacring, enslaving, or expelling its non-Christian inhabitants—Jews and Muslims alike. But the Crusades rapidly degenerated into intra-Christian wars, for Europeans were just as eager to seize and plunder the lands of Christian Byzantium as the Muslim Turks had been.[59] It is ironic that in doing so, the Christian West set the stage for the eventual collapse of the Byzantine empire and its loss to the Ottoman Turks. In 1187, Saladin defeated the Crusaders at the Battle of Hattin and recaptured Jerusalem.[60] In the Third Crusade, Saladin's troops surrendered, in a stalemate, to Richard I ("the Lion-Hearted") on the Mediterranean at the city of Acre in 1191. They divided up the territory, with Muslims keeping Jerusalem but promising to accommodate Christian pilgrims.

THE MONGOLS

The Crusaders did not terminate the Abbasid Caliphate and the Muslim Golden Age. It in fact ended in 1258, when Baghdad was destroyed by the Mongol hordes, among the world's most brutal conquerors, who created the biggest empire in history. Their territory extended at various times to Eastern Europe, China, Korea, Mongolia, Persia, Turkestan, Armenia, Russia, Burma, Vietnam, and Thailand. Before reaching Baghdad, the Mongols had already destroyed many Muslim cities under the ruthless and skilled leadership of Genghis Khan and his descendants. To encourage their foes to surrender without a fight, the Mongols used state-of-the-art military tactics that included the destruction of all stored grain, the obliteration of irrigation systems, the razing of cities and towns, the systematic massacre of local populations, the stacking of victims' skulls in huge pyramids, and the use of civilian prisoners as human shields—and even as human bridges, to enable Mongols to cross moats of besieged cities.

The Mongol invasion was so catastrophic that it created a sense of doomsday for Muslims; after all, the faithful were being crushed by "infidels," creating a great crisis of confidence. At the same time, some historians have argued, after initially paralyzing Muslim societies the Mongol invasions provided a long period of peace—the so-called Pax Mongolica—across a vast stretch of territory that allowed the resilient Muslim societies not only to re-emerge but to flourish.[61] Following their conquests, the Mongols rebuilt many Muslim cities, created dazzling courts, and to some degree picked up where the Abbasids, Fatimids, and Umayyads had left off in promoting science, art, and scholarship.

Indeed, it is one of history's great landmarks that the Mongols converted to Islam—a conversion that saved the Muslim power and realms from fading into history. Their conversion was also relatively swift. By the early fourteenth century, most of the Mongol realms had adopted Islam.[62]

Rise and Fall of the Ottomans

The emergence of European commercial and political power in the Mediterranean region in the fifteenth century coincided with the rise of the Muslim Ottoman empire. The Ottomans became the most powerful western Muslim rulers, capturing Constantinople in 1453. They won battles with a highly trained corps of converted slaves and new weapons that used gunpowder. In their march through the fifteenth and sixteenth centuries, the Ottomans conquered Egypt, Syria, Hungary, Cyprus, and Rhodes, eventually creating one of the largest empires in history.

Coinciding with the rise of the Ottoman empire, from the fifteenth century through the seventeenth century, two other Islamic empires emerged: the Safavids in Iran and the Mughals (Persian for Mongols) in India. Other emergent powers included the sultans of Morocco and the Uzbeks in Central Asia. Within these realms, too, semi-independent dynasties emerged in the regions of the Caspian Sea, the Black Sea, Central Asia, Afghanistan, India, and equatorial Africa. The key point is that even at the height of Muslim power, there was no single Muslim umma, or community; the Turkish, Arabic, Iranian, and Indian realms had divided Islam politically, culturally, and economically, retaining only the unity of the fundamental precepts and Five Pillars of Islam.

The first major manifestation of Muslim military weakness occurred in 1571, when Spanish and Venetian fleets defeated the

Akbar the Great

The emperor Akbar the Great (1543–1605), generally considered the greatest of the Mughal emperors, is best known for his religious tolerance. He abolished the jizya, the tax on non-Muslims, built his capital around the tomb of a Sufi saint, invited theologians from other faiths to discussions, and married two Hindu princesses. "No man should be interfered with on account of his religion," Akbar once said. He even promoted an ecumenical faith that blended Islam, Brahmanism, Christianity, and Zoroastrianism, but it did not catch on, and he himself died a Muslim.[1]

1. See Vincent Smith, *Akbar, the Great Moghul* (Oxford University Press, 1917), p. 257. See also "Akbar the Great" (www.kamat.com/kalranga/mogul/akbar.htm).

Ottomans in a naval battle off Lepanto, Greece—a victory that was captured in heroic paintings by Tintoretto and Veronese. The second major failure was the Turks' unsuccessful siege of Vienna in 1683. However, the empire's actual disintegration began with its first territorial concession, in the 1699 Treaty of Carlowicz, when it ceded Hungary to Austria. In 1774 the Treaty of Küçük Kaynarca was imposed on the empire by Russia, and an 1802 treaty with France reaffirmed earlier concessions.[63] The loss of territory was not so significant, however, as the fact that it was with these treaties that the European powers first began to obtain economic, commercial, and political concessions from the Ottoman empire (and similar concessions were eventually wrested from the Iranian and Mughal empires). These concessions, known later as capitulations, became the engine of Europe's political, economic, and military domination of the Muslim realms. European nation-states were also gaining dominance by modernizing their economies, using new military technologies, and centralizing their political authority.

From the eighteenth century on, then, one sees the gradual stagnation or decline of all three remaining Muslim empires, which were hamstrung by their increasing insularity, their inability to control the flow of trade along international trade routes, and their limited ability to take advantage of technological innovation during the Industrial Revolution. Through invasion, colonization, or economic dominance, the British established control over much of India, the Russians defeated the Ottomans in Crimea, and France occupied Egypt.[64] The first two major challenges against the Ottoman empire in the Middle East were Napoleon's invasion of Egypt in 1798 and the French occupation of Algeria in 1830.[65]

Many other factors contributed to the decline of the Ottoman empire and there are a number of theories about why it eventually fell:

—The decline of the effectiveness of the Sultans and the quality of their administrations. While the early centuries of the Ottoman empire were marked by some extremely able and sometimes brilliant leaders, this was not the case in the later years, when its rulers lacked the ability and strategic foresight of their predecessors. Among Ottoman rulers, there also developed a sense of complacency and a belief in the infallibility of Ottoman institutions and the inferiority of the "infidels."

—A population explosion, which could not be supported by the land available for cultivation, along with the failure of land reforms that resulted in peasant unrest and social and economic disruption.

—The failure of the empire to integrate various nations, peoples, and regions into a cohesive whole. As a result, the empire remained a collection of different ethnic and religious populations (*millets*)—Greek Orthodox, Armenian, and Jewish—as well as semiautonomous regions—Arabia, Lebanon, North Africa, among others—without a common, unifying identity or unity of purpose.

—Financial and economic crises at the beginning of the sixteenth century, which led to the depreciation and debasement of the currency, high inflation, and unemployment.

—The inability of native merchants in the empire to compete effectively with European joint stock companies that had long-term strategies, as well as reserves and the political muscle of the European powers, behind them.

—The decline of the empire's military forces.

—The lack of development of cities to serve as economic centers and a base for the rise of a middle class.

—Perhaps most important of all, the rise of nineteenth-century nationalism in all regions of the Ottoman empire, involving Christians at first, and later even Muslims, such as Arabs and Turks.[66]

By the early twentieth century, Britain, France, Russia, and the Netherlands ruled over nearly all Muslim societies, with only Afghanistan, Iran, and a much reduced Ottoman empire retaining their independence.[67]

TWO

Clash of Modernists and Traditionalists

THE DECLINE OF Muslim realms created another crisis of confidence and raised many questions. How should Muslims challenge European colonialism so as to regain, or retain, their independence and political and economic viability? The debate divided along two basic lines: On one side, some argued that the decline was caused by moral laxity and the departure from the true path of Islam; these traditionalists called for an Islamic revival. On the other side, there were those who claimed that Islamic societies had not suddenly declined but had long faltered, owing to a chronic failure to modernize their societies and institutions; these reformers said Muslim societies could be rescued only by modernizing and challenging the West on its own terms. Each option had its own risks. Looking to the past for answers risked greater stagnation. Looking to the future risked the loss of indigenous culture: was it possible to modernize without Westernizing? The contest between these two responses still shakes the Muslim realms.

The historian Arnold Toynbee attempted to encapsulate the essence of this conflict between modernists and traditionalists, not only in Muslim societies but in all societies. In his twelve-volume *A Study of History*, Toynbee refers to modernists and traditionalists, respectively, as "Herodians" and "Zealots," terms borrowed from the Jewish experience. In his theory of history, civilizations rise when people make creative responses to a variety of challenges—geographic, economic, political, and spiritual—and their continuing creativity sustains their civilizations. He theorizes that civilizations fall in a downward spiral when creativity falters, challenges are not met, anarchy develops, and tyrants take charge. Ultimately, these declining civilizations are threatened by more creative and dynamic ones. In response, the threatened people typically follow one of two basic paths: If the Zealot leaders prevail, the civilization responds by isolating itself and trying to revive ideas and practices from an idealized past. If Herodians take the lead, the civilization responds by borrowing its opponents' best tools, synthesizing their best ideas, and using the new tools and ideas to compete and regain strength and control. Naturally, in his view, successful civilizations are those that accept the Herodian challenge, while others ossify or decline.[1]

Of course, not everyone agrees with Toynbee's crystallization of history into two forces—and certainly Zealots, or traditionalists, do not. But Toynbee is insightful in describing the intense struggles between modernism and traditionalism in Muslim societies that have occurred, on and off, for more than a century. Moreover, both modernists and traditionalists look at the entire history of Islam, rationalizing past successes and failures in ways that bolster their current theological, ideological, and political stances.

The Struggle against Colonialism

Until the nineteenth century, the Muslim struggle against colonial powers was considered the domain of secular political authorities, but gradually the struggle was joined by so-called national liberation movements. For while Europe exported colonialism and imperialism to Muslim realms, it could not avoid also exporting the ideas and legacies of the Enlightenment, nationalism, and European institutions and political movements—liberal, conservative, and radical. As such, the colonialists sowed the seeds of anticolonial movements, which used European ideologies against European dominance. Indeed, generations of nationalist leaders in the Middle East and North Africa were educated in European and even American institutions of higher education—including the American University of Beirut, founded in 1866, and the American University of Cairo, founded in 1919.

It is also not surprising that Muslim nationalists attempted to use Islam and the ulama as organizing tools to mobilize their societies against the colonial powers. (After all, the colonial powers themselves used religion as an effective tool to undermine nationalist and anticolonial movements.) Naturally, these alliances proved to be only temporary and expedient, especially because nationalism was then a new and not well-understood concept—and a secular one at that. The idea of a secular nation, separate from the religious community, the umma, was in theory alien to Islam. But even though religion and state were not explicitly separated, they had been administered separately by Caliphs and the ulama for centuries.[2] Yet in their shared effort to combat colonialism and imperialism, the ulama and other traditionalists periodically marched under the banner of nationalism. As a result, across colonized Muslim societies Islamic revivals proliferated—and while they energized nationalist movements, they also empowered the ulama. Hence, anticolonialism sometimes took on a religious fervor, which Muslim reformers have often been unable to moderate; mobilizing the ulama has been easy, demobilizing them has proven difficult.

Muslim history and theology provided both the necessary language and the justification for a struggle against the European intruders. Muhammad had preached that the umma, the Muslim community, must be totally focused on *jihad* (meaning "to struggle") to live in the way God intended, as laid out in the Qur'an. Throughout Muslim history, the concept of jihad has been used to encourage piety among individuals as well as to wage war to defend the faith or convert "infidels." If there was prosperity in the umma, it indicated that Muslims were living according to God's will; if the umma declined, it was a sign that they had strayed from the Qur'an. Any attack on this religious community, from within or without, was considered an act of blasphemy or an act of aggression that must be checked through jihad.[3]

At the same time, some nineteenth-century Islamic movements were more interested in reviving Islam than in overthrowing colonial rule elsewhere. Such was the case with Sunni *Wahhabis*, members of a puritanical denomination in the Arabian peninsula. Named after the eighteenth-century reformer Muhammad ibn Abd al-Wahhab, they also called themselves *Muwahhidun*, Unitarians. They condemned many modern innovations and advocated a strict and literal adherence to the Qur'an and hadith in an effort to return to Islam as they believed it was practiced in the seventh century, and thus recapture the strength Islam had given

Just War

When it comes to preaching about war, the Abrahamic faiths are nearly on the same page, according to some scholars. Muhammad's approach to war had much in common with ancient Jewish traditions and with the fourth century writings of St. Augustine. In the *City of God*, St. Augustine wrote that war—when conducted in a manner that limits harm and shows mercy to the vanquished—can be justified by the overarching need of a legitimate authority to preserve peace, protect the innocent, repulse invasion, or reclaim territory. James Turner Johnson, author of *Just War and Jihad: Historical and Theoretical Perspectives on War and Peace in Western and Islamic Traditions,* notes that Islamic and Christian traditions, as well as international law, agree on the principles of just war and its practice: "There is no culture conflict here."[1]

The author Amir Taheri, however, maintains that the Christian idea of a just or holy war has been mistakenly grafted onto Islam by other Islamic scholars. "No war is either holy or just in Islam," he writes. "War is allowed if it is waged in defense of the faith, against a tyrant *(taghut)* or to rescue a Muslim people from repression by infidels. But even then, the rules, and the limits *(hoddod)*, that apply to all actions, apply to war: The intention must be pure, the method must not be excessive, the change must not be worse than the status quo."[2]

1. See Pew Forum on Religion and Public Life, "Just War Tradition and the New War on Terrorism: A Discussion of the Origins and Precepts of Just War Principles and Their Application to a War on Terrorism," December 2001 (http://pewforum.org/publications).

2. Amir Taheri, "Islam and War," February 16, 2003 (www.benadorassociates. com/pf.php?id+233).

to the early Muslims.[4] The teachings of Muhammad ibn Abd al-Wahhab represent the strictest interpretations of the Hanbali school.

In India, the most influential advocate of traditionalism was the Deoband school. Known formally as Darul Uloom Deoband and named after its location in northern India, near Delhi, the school is considered by some to be second only to Al-Azhar in Cairo as the most important center of traditional Islamic studies. The Deoband school was established in 1866 by Maulana Mohammed Qasim Nanauti to preserve the Muslim heritage against the encroachments of British colonialism. Yet the school grew from its orthodox Wahhabi beginnings into a more modern institution, exhibiting sharp differences with other Muslim traditionalists—and even with its own offshoots in other countries. The Deoband school, for example, supported India's secular constitution and religious pluralism. The school also opposed the partition of the Indian subcontinent and the creation of a Muslim homeland in Pakistan. As Marghboor Rahman, the seminary's vice chancellor, recently put it, "We are Indians first, then Muslims."[5]

SELF-DETERMINATION MOVEMENTS OF ALL KINDS

Nationalist movements in the nineteenth century were not confined to ruling ethnic majorities in Muslim empires; minorities soon became enthused with their own nationalist aspirations as well. It is not surprising, therefore, to see Greeks, Albanians, Armenians, Macedonians, Serbs, and Bulgarians adopting nationalism as a revolutionary movement in pursuit of a national reformation, autonomy, or even independence from the Ottoman empire. Nationalism was an equal opportunity ideology. It was welcomed not only by non-Muslim ethnic groups, but also by minority ethnic groups of Muslims who attempted to find autonomy or independence. Following the Greeks' success in winning independence in 1830, all the others headed toward autonomy.

Far more controversial, however, was the rise of nationalism among Arabs, Turks, and other majority ethnic groups, who were Muslims. Such a development posed a great challenge to the concept of a single Muslim umma with a single ruler. But nationalism—with its emphasis on the importance of shared language, culture, religion, history, and homeland—was considered a legitimate aspiration for Muslims, who saw it as a force that would assist them in keeping their communities together and liberating their societies from colonial powers. In an effort to reconcile nationalism with the concept of a single umma, the proponents of nationalism rationalized that it was not an end in itself, but rather, a means to build a new umma—one that would eventually be a confederacy of independent, free, and equal member states. In this way, nationalism was not considered a rejection of the umma, but a redefinition.

Moreover, in some of these nationalist struggles even Christians and Muslims joined together, transcending their religious differences to form new states or secular political parties. There was growing awareness of past glories and talk about "historical mission," destiny, and the uniqueness of native languages. People saw themselves not just as a religious community, but as a one that shared distinct cultural, ethnic, geographic, and historical bonds. In Syria, Christians and Muslims cooperated to forge a national identity based on their common Arabic language and culture; similarly in Egypt, Coptic Christians and Muslims together created a nationalist identity based on their love of the land and centuries of overlapping pharaonic, Christian, and Muslim cultures.

Even conservative Muslims were reminded that there were historical precedents for bringing together such heterogeneous communities—after all, the Prophet Muhammad's first umma in Medina included pagan, Jewish, and Muslim members. India, too, saw interfaith nationalist coalitions: in the political sphere, the Hindu-dominated Congress Party included many prominent Muslim leaders who shared the aspiration for an independent India and opposed partition along religious lines.

SECULAR EFFORTS TO CREATE UNITY FLOUNDER

Not only does one see the emergence of secular nationalist movements that challenged European colonialists, but also the emergence of secular "pan-" movements in Muslim realms between the 1870s and 1918. These movements were similar to the Pan-German and Pan-Slav movements in that they attempted to unite ethnic groups that shared a "common blood," language, or culture. They included Pan-Turkism, which was an effort to unite all Turkish-speaking peoples, and Pan-Iranism, which was a movement to unite all Persian-speaking peoples. Reaching still further, others called for a Pan-Islamism, a secular movement that could bridge both secular and religious aspirations of Muslims worldwide.[6] To Muslim modernists, these movements were organizing tools to promote political freedom and create large ethnic units that might give them access to resources, natural and other, for greater economic and military strength. But to the ulama and other traditionalists who supported these movements, they were merely expedient vehicles for unifying the religious community to recreate the umma as a theocracy.

Sayyid Jamal ad-Din al-Afghani, an Iranian scholar and political activist, was the first theoretician of Pan-Islamism and Muslim modernism, which was a blend of Pan-Islamism, secularism, and nationalism.[7] Al-Afghani had seriously challenged the authorities, both Muslim and European, from the 1870s.[8] He had warned about "the danger of European intervention, the need for national unity to resist it, the need for a broader unity of the Islamic peoples [and] the need for a constitution to limit the ruler's power." He ascribed the decline of Muslim power to a combination of European imperialism, autocratic Muslim rulers, and a retrogressive ulama that saw no place for Islam in the modern world. Al-Afghani called for engaging as well as confronting the West, creating Muslim-style democracies, and reforming Islam—to encourage the creation of new ideas, much as Muslim peoples had done during the Golden Age of science and learning in the Abbasid period.[9] In a "Lecture on Teaching and Learning," given in 1882 in Calcutta, al-Afghani said:

The strangest thing of all is that our ulama these days have divided science into two parts. One they call Muslim science, and one European science. Because of this they forbid others to teach some of the useful sciences. They have not understood that science is that noble thing that has no connection with any nation, and is not distinguished by anything but itself. Rather, everything that is known is known by science, and every nation that becomes renowned becomes renowned through science. ... The Islamic religion is the closest of religions to science and knowledge, and there is no incompatibility between science and knowledge and the foundation of the Islamic faith.[10]

These modernist ideas were not confined to the Ottoman empire or to the Indian subcontinent, Iran, or Russia. They even flourished in such isolated lands as Afghanistan, where Mahmud Tarzi, a modernist who published the first Afghan newspaper— *Siraj al-Akhbar Afghaniyah* (the Lamp of the News of Afghanistan)—argued in 1911 that European colonists were pursuing policies that propagated materialism and were designed to sap the strength of Islam. To this end, he said, colonists supported the activities of Christian missionaries, capitalized on and even promoted divisions among the Muslims, and instituted educational programs that were aimed at stifling the revival of Islam.[11]

In Tarzi's view, Muslims needed to protect their common heritage by closing ranks behind unified political, cultural, economic, and military strategies. He and others were inspired by Japan's stunning defeat of its far more powerful adversary in the Russo-Japanese War of 1904–05. They reasoned that if a nation like Japan, which lacked many natural resources, could nearly annihilate the Russians' Baltic fleet and defeat its army in Manchuria, then there was hope that Muslim nations, working together in a disciplined way, could recapture their autonomy and power from the Europeans.

The Postcolonial Struggle

During the colonial period, Muslim elites—the rationalists, secularists, and modernists, however one might describe them—attempted to build an infrastructure for modern statehood in anticipation of the eventual liberation of their lands. But they had an uphill struggle. Efforts to modernize Muslim economies during colonial periods were skewed by the needs of the Europeans, who sought raw materials for European factories and a growing colonial market for finished products. In addition, there were internal conflicts, such as the ulama's opposition to modern banking, based on the Qur'anic ban on charging interest. As a result, Muslim countries, not unlike others in Asia and Africa, were unable to meet the multiple challenges of the Industrial Revolution and its aftermath. Muslim nations lacked the capital, among other things, to modernize rapidly. In one instance, Egypt was headed for insolvency after completing an ambitious program—which included building the Suez Canal, 900 miles of railway, and vast irrigation projects. Its precarious financial situation gave Britain, which had a controlling interest in the Suez Canal, a reason to protect its investments by occupying the country in 1882.[12] It was not until 1956 that Britain removed all of its troops from Egypt.

Since the nineteenth century, in spite of the debates between modernists and traditionalists, many modern Muslim states have emerged—complete, of course, with museums, libraries, hospitals, schools, universities, and urban skyscrapers, including the world's tallest buildings, in Kuala Lumpur. The record shows that

Islam is not averse to science or technology.[13] The problem is that there are not enough resources to provide Muslim populations with equal opportunities in education and employment and not enough political resilience in many governments to allow the people to participate in the political process. The debate is also about values—how to protect a society's cultural heritage and traditional practices in an age of globalization and how to develop a creative coexistence between modernism and traditionalism without Westernization.

Overall, most Muslim nations are considered developing nations. Despite countless attempts to modernize along Western models through the twentieth century, most Muslim societies have not been able to surmount barriers in worldwide economic competition. A major problem for modernizers, right up to the present day, has been the structure of the education systems. While colonial governments established some Western-style schools, many traditional Muslims responded by expanding religious schools, often with strictly religious curricula.[14] Most rudimentary Muslim religious school systems have long relied on rote learning and have concentrated on the fundamentals of Islamic culture and religion, often excluding from the curriculum math, science, history, languages, and foreign literature—in short, taking an approach to knowledge that completely ignores the tradition dating back to Islam's Golden Age, when Muslims embraced knowledge as universal, not owned by separate peoples or countries.

To put the problems faced by Muslim societies in perspective, one should remember that the problems they confronted, and still do confront, were not endemic to Muslim societies. Japan, Korea, China, and other societies in the seventeenth through the nineteenth centuries faced similar challenges. They blamed their decline in power on the West, rejected modernism, and sought isolationism as the best way to preserve independence as well as their historical legacies. In Japan, for example, it was not until the Meiji Restoration in 1868 that modernization and Westernization began to take place. It is also interesting to note that Japan's intellectual dependence on the West lasted for only a generation after European-style universities had been imported.[15]

Today, many Muslims are cognizant of the shortcomings in their institutional development, economies, social progress, and systems of education. Mohamed Charfi, a former minister of education in Tunisia (which began modernizing its educational system and curricula in 1989) writes of primitive religious education in Muslim countries: "The consequences of such teachings on the minds of young people in most Muslim-majority countries have been disastrous." In some societies such schools also exclude girls and women, which of course deals a major blow to economic and social development—not to mention to women's rights and the stewardship of the next generation of children.

Muslim countries have also been hamstrung by a shortage of quality institutions of higher education, especially their lack of modern universities with state-of-the-art scientific laboratories and appropriate faculty to train scientists. The combination of these factors has resulted in a woefully inadequate number of scientists in Muslim countries—by one recent estimate, less than 1 percent of the world's scientists are Muslims, even though Muslims account for almost 20 percent of the world's population.[16] The situation is aggravated by Muslim countries that send students abroad to study, as most of these students do not return,

Education and Its Abuses

Mohamed Charfi, former education minister of Tunisia, describes the dangers of traditional education in Muslim countries today: "Students learn that, in order to be good believers, they should be living under a Caliph, that divine law makes it necessary to stone the adulterer and forbid lending at interest . . . only to discover, out in the street, a society directed by a civil government with a modern penal code and an economy founded on a banking system. Many Muslim children still learn at school the ancient ideology of a triumphant Muslim empire, an ideology that held all non-Muslims to be in error and saw its mission as bringing Islam's light to the world. And yet young people see their governments working to live in peace with non-Muslim powers. Such discordant teachings do not prepare children to live in a changing world. Osama bin Laden, like the 15 Saudis who participated in the criminal operations of Sept. 11, seems to be have been the pure product of his schooling. While Saudi Arabia is officially a moderate state allied with America, it has also been one of the main supporters of Islamic fundamentalism by financing schools following the Wahhabi doctrine. Saudi-backed madrasas [religious schools] in Pakistan and Afghanistan have played significant roles in the strengthening of radical Islam in those countries."[1] Indeed, at the Darul Uloom Haqqania religious school in Nowshera, Pakistan, Chancellor Moulana Samiul-Haq noted in 1998: "Each and every person in this institution wants to be like Osama bin Laden." The school trained most of the Taliban leaders.[2]

Widespread Illiteracy, Limited Higher Education

According to a recent report on education in the twenty-two member states of the Arab League, of a combined population of 240.7 million (in 1999), 68 million were illiterate.[3] In 1997, these states had a total of only 175 universities, of which 128 were run by governments. Of the 175 universities, 108 were established between 1981 and 1996, and about half of those were in just three nations: Sudan, Jordan, and Yemen. The cost of education per student in 1995–96 averaged $2,444 a year in the twenty-two states, ranging from a high of $15,701 in Oman to a low of $515 in Yemen.

"Many of the universities have barely taken off; many are poorly staffed, ill-equipped, and can barely qualify for the name; many government ones were opened for political reasons, and most of the private [ones] for profit," the report states. The curriculum is often limited: in Saudi Arabia the most common field of study is Islamic law, there are no college programs for general law, business, or political science, and opportunities to study the humanities are "very rare."

Altogether, the Arab states had more than 3 million students in higher education during 1996; the vast majority were in bachelor-level programs, and about 12 percent were in two- or three-year programs at technical institutes. Some old universities, like Alexandria in Egypt, are huge: 130,000 students were enrolled in 1995–96. The number of students attending college has increased significantly since 1990: in 1997 the "gross enrollment ratio" (not defined in the report) was 17.3 percent for the male secondary student population and 12.4 percent for female students, compared to the world's "more developed regions" (not specified), where the ratios were 56.8 percent for the male student population and 65.6 percent for female students.

1. Mohamed Charfi, "Reaching the Next Muslim Generation," *New York Times*, March 12, 2002, p. A27.

2. Andrew Maykuth, "The Taliban's Version of Harvard: 'Each and Every Person in This Institution Wants to Be Like Osama bin Laden,'" *Gazette* (Montreal), September 5, 1998.

3. Regional Office for Education in the Arab States, "Higher Education in the Arab States" (Beirut: February 2002).

causing a brain drain—as well as lost opportunities for bringing new ideas back to their Muslim homelands. There is no doubt that the educational systems of all Muslim countries need to be strengthened and modernized, which includes encouraging academic freedom for teaching and research.[17]

A group of Muslim scholars recently issued a landmark study about the dire situation in Arab societies. "The Arab Human Development Report 2002" was published in June by the United Nations Development Program and the Arab Fund for Economic and Social Development. It is important to note that the study represents the "unbiased, objective analysis" of "a group of distinguished Arab intellectuals"—nearly thirty scholars in Islamic sociology, economics, and culture. It was written by Nader Fergany, a prominent labor economist in Egypt. The project's advisory board included Thoraya Obaid, a Saudi who heads the UN Population Fund; Mervat Tallawy, an Egyptian diplomat; and Clovis Maksoud, who heads the Center for the Global South at American University in Washington. Some of the scholars' assessments about the status of twenty-two Arab nations:

Intellectual and cultural isolation. Arab publishers translate into Arabic only about 330 books a year, or one-fifth the number that the Greeks translate into Greek. To put this in perspective, during the past 1,000 years, the entire Arab world has translated into Arabic only as many books as Spanish publishers now annually translate into Spanish. There is also a "severe shortage" of new writing by Arabs. Filmmaking is declining. Internet use is low, lower even than in sub-Saharan Africa, and only about 1 in 100 Arabs has a personal computer.

Minimal research and development. With Arab nations accounting for less than one-seventh of the world's average annual investment in research, in relation to the size of overall national economies Arab achievements in science and technology are very limited.

Declining productivity. The growth in per capita income has been stalled for two decades, at a level just above that of sub-Saharan Africa. About 15 percent of the labor force was unemployed. Forty years ago, Arab productivity was 32 percent of the North American level; by 1990, it had fallen to 19 percent.

Inadequate education. While Arab nations spend more on education than other countries in the developing world, more than one in four Arabs is illiterate, and half of Arab women cannot read or write. About 10 million children (six to fifteen years old) do not go to school. Worse still, "There is evidence that the quality of education has deteriorated."

Human resources squandered. Women are routinely denied advancement in the workplace. "Sadly, the Arab world is depriving itself of the creativity and productivity of half of its citizens."

Poverty of opportunities. Due to its overall oil wealth, the Arab region has the (developing) world's lowest level of abject poverty (measured as incomes of less than $1 a day), yet more than one in five Arabs lives on less than $2 a day. "The Arab region is hobbled by a different kind of poverty—poverty of capabilities and poverty of opportunities."

Freedom denied. According to two international indexes widely used to compare levels of freedom—including free speech, civil rights, political rights, freedom of the press, and government accountability—the Arab region has the lowest level of freedom of any of the world's seven regions. "The attitudes of public authorities range from opposition to manipulation to 'freedom under surveillance.'" The report also noted that "the wave of democracy that transformed governance in most of Latin America and East Asia in the 1980s and early 1990s has barely reached the Arab states. This freedom deficit undermines human development."

High maternal mortality. The death rate for women during childbirth is four times worse than in East Asia. At the same time, birth rates are soaring. Currently, the twenty-two Arab states have a total population of 280 million; that is projected to grow to between 410 million and 459 million by 2020. Today, 38 percent of Arabs are under fourteen years old.

Disaffected youth. Half of Arab youths say they want to emigrate. The scholars conclude:

What the region needs to ensure a bright future for coming generations is the political will to invest in Arab capabilities and knowledge, particularly those of Arab women, in good governance, and in strong cooperation between Arab nations. . . . The Arab world is at a crossroads. The fundamental choice is whether its trajectory will remain marked by inertia . . . and by ineffective policies that have produced the substantial development challenges facing the region; or whether prospects for an Arab renaissance, anchored in human development, will be actively pursued.[18]

THREE

Challenges of the Twentieth Century

WORLD WAR I, in a dramatic way, once again confirmed the answer to the big question: is there a single, unified "Muslim world"—with one umma, under one Caliph, that transcends political and religious divisions in all Muslim realms? The stage was set in 1914, when the Young Turks of the Ottoman empire joined the Central Powers (the German and Austro-Hungarian empires) against the Allied Powers (Britain, France, and Russia).

On November 25, 1914, shortly after declaring war against the Allied Powers, the Caliph, Sultan Mehmed V (1844–1918), called for Muslims worldwide to join the Ottomans in their own jihad, or holy war. The proclamation stated: "The Muslims in general who are under the oppressive grasp of the aforesaid tyrannical governments in such places as the Crimea, Kazan, Turkestan, Bukhara, Khiva, and India, and those dwelling in China, Afghanistan, Africa, and other regions of the earth, are hastening to join in this Great Jihad to the best of their ability, with life and property, alongside the Ottomans, in conformity with the relevant holy Fatwas."[1]

The Caliph's *fatwa* (legal decree) failed. The monolithic unity of Islam appeared to be only an idealistic abstraction. National, ethnic, dynastic, regional, cultural, class, and tribal interests proved stronger than the majestic appeal of the Caliph. Not only did Muslims outside the empire fight *against* the Ottomans in the ranks of their enemies—the British and French forces and their allies—but there was also a revolt of Muslims *within* the empire. Pursuing ethnic, dynastic, and even religious agendas, Muslims in Arabia—including *Hashemites*, the traditional guardians of Islam's holy sites, and   Wahhabis—revolted against the Ottoman Turks, charging them with the corruption of Islam.

In the aftermath of World War I, the last major symbol—or relic—of unity among all Muslim societies passed out of existence. The Caliphate, which had in theory linked Muslims worldwide to Muhammad since his death in 632, was formally abolished in 1924, under the leadership of Mustafa Kemal Atatürk, founder and first president of modern Turkey.[2] Subsequent efforts organized in India and elsewhere, to restore the Caliphate failed.

The Interwar Period

Following World War I and the defeat of the Ottoman empire, the struggle between modernists and traditionalists unfolded. On the modernist side, some secularized states emerged. One was the Republic of Turkey, where Atatürk plunged ahead with modernizing and secularizing the country along Western lines. Islamic law was replaced with Belgian and Swiss civil codes, religious schools were closed, the Sufi order was banned, the Gregorian calendar was adopted, the Roman alphabet replaced the Arabic, and citizens were even required to wear Western dress. While Turkey's secular transition was abrupt and comprehensive, most postcolonial Muslim nations kept European-style, secular legal institutions, and Islamic law generally applied only to family law and ritual. Also held over were the colonists' languages: French in North Africa and Lebanon, for example, and English in India, Asia, and Malaysia.[3]

Modernization was pursued elsewhere, as in Iran. After a successful constitutional movement and armed struggle, in 1906 Iranian reformers had secured a constitutional monarchy under the reign of Muzaffar al-Din Shah and they fought to preserve it under his successors. Following World War I, Reza Shah Pahlavi established a new dynasty in 1925 and imposed a version of the draconian formula for modernization used by Atatürk in Turkey. The Shah's aim was to make Iran a modern, secular state. He, too, imposed Western dress codes as well as a secular constitution, a national banking system, a modern army, and compulsory education. He revised laws based on French criminal codes and Belgian commercial regulations. He also opened modern schools and the University of Teheran. But the Shah kept the Arabic script and the Muslim calendar. He built museums, libraries, and other cultural institutions to preserve Iran's Persian heritage, as distinct from that of the Turks or Arabs. In order to Westernize without opposition from the ulama, he coopted them through financial subsidies and administrative appointments—and occasionally did away with resistant clerics. His policies were continued under his son, Muhammad Reza Shah Pahlavi.

On the traditionalist side, Saudi Arabia emerged as one model for a religious state. In 1932, Abdul-Aziz ibn Saud united four tribal provinces to create the Kingdom of Saudi Arabia—a monarchy that uses the Qur'an and its injunctions for social and economic equality to serve as the nation's constitution.[4] Most of its citizens are members of the orthodox Wahhabi sect of Sunni Muslims. Islam is also the official religion in a handful of states, including Jordan, Iran, Yemen, Morocco, Kuwait, and Egypt. It is worth noting, however, that most of the world's Muslims live in secular states with varying degrees of separation between state and mosque.[5]

Elusive Unity

Following World War II, the United Nations in 1946 ended the mandate system, which had left the territories of the defeated powers in World War I under the mandate, or direction, of the victors until they were deemed ready to govern themselves. When the UN recognized independent states in Syria, Lebanon, and Jordan, there was an opportunity for secularism with a modernist agenda to emerge as the dominant force. That was not to be, however, as the partition of Palestine to create the state of Israel in 1948 opened a new chapter of conflict in Middle East politics, as well as in Muslim politics more generally, unleashing contending dynastic, secular, nationalist, and religious forces.

But even though Israel emerged as a polarizing force, there was often more outrage than unity, indicating that nationalist, ethnic, regional, and cultural divisions were deeper than any cohesive impulse. The Arab League, which was created in 1945, could not manage these international forces or overcome many differences within Arab nations. While it became a symbol of unity, it was not effective at creating unity. The Arab League was to be the forerunner of a Pan-Arab movement; several states and various political parties did make strides to form regional, political, economic, and military alliances, but those efforts were nearly all unsuccessful.

For example, in 1958 a number of Arab states decided to form political mergers, yet they quickly fell apart. These included the United Arab Republic, consisting of Syria, Egypt, and Yemen, which lasted only three years (though Egypt used the name until 1971); and the Arab Federation, consisting of Iraq and Jordan, which lasted about six months before ethnic and dynastic interests tore it apart. In 1964 there was an abortive plan to unite Algeria, Libya, Morocco, and Tunisia in an economic counterpart to the European common market. Even collaborative Muslim efforts suffered from disunity. Shared national interests brought Egypt, Jordan, and Syria together to join forces against Israel in the Six-Day War of 1967. Their unity was short-lived, and the war ended with a victorious Israel occupying the Golan Heights, the West Bank, Gaza, Sinai, and East Jerusalem.

This defeat and loss of territory, known as the Disaster, did not unify Muslim nations, but sowed the seeds of further disunity. It also reopened the debate between modernists and traditionalists as to what was the best way to combat not only Israel, but also Western influence. Modernists contended that the defeat demonstrated the need to shift modernization efforts into high gear. Traditionalists argued that the defeat highlighted the shortcomings of secular nationalism, as well as the limits to relying on Western technologies and institutions as models for organizing and defending Muslim societies. True unity, they argued, could be accomplished only through a religious revival.

Moreover, the position of the ulama (clerics in the religious establishment) was strengthened during the cold war. They received support from conservative, secular, Muslim nations as well as Western powers, both of which considered the ulama bulwarks against communism. The ulama received additional support from the West, which denounced the Soviet Union for denying Muslims in Central Asia and elsewhere the freedom to practice their religion. Not only was it in the West's interests to mobilize Muslim states against the Soviets and communism, it was also in the ulama's interest to oppose the godless "evil empire." These combined efforts lent legitimacy to the ulama and eventually contributed to their militancy.

But even while the ulama flourished, nearly all efforts at unity, political or religious, continued to flounder. Only one tiny union from the postwar period has survived: the United Arab Emirates, created in 1971–72, with territory about the size of South Carolina. Since the 1970s, no other attempt has succeeded. The aborted efforts include the Federation of Arab Republics, consisting of Libya, Egypt, and Syria, in 1972; a plan to merge Egypt and Libya in 1973; and Libyan proposals to merge with Tunisia in 1974, Chad in 1981, Morocco in 1984, Algeria in 1987, and the Sudan in 1990.[6] Instead, Arab states fought among themselves for territory, wealth, and power—most notably in the Iran-Iraq war of 1980–88. During the Persian Gulf war, as well, most Arab states fought Iraq under the UN banner, and there were no Muslim allies in Iraqi trenches.

The fragmentation of unity was not confined to Arab nations: there were similar divisions in the Indian subcontinent during its partition. There were Muslims who wanted a unified secular India, others who wanted a Muslim homeland—either for religious reasons or out of fear that they would face discrimination by a Hindu majority after India became independent.[7] The British-sponsored partition of the Indian subcontinent in 1947 gave Muslims a homeland in the Islamic Republic of Pakistan—but left more than 100 million Muslims in India. Although religion once again was used to rally support for the partition, Pakistan was founded and organized as a completely secular state—and to emphasize that, the word *Islamic* was removed from Pakistan's official name in 1962. The partition, of course, was troubled from the start. Sir Cyril Radcliffe, who had never previously visited India, was given only five weeks to draw new national boundaries across a vast and bitterly disputed territory. The division created a new nation, but one with two land masses that were separated by 1,000 miles of Indian territory: West Pakistan, located in the northwestern corner of the Indian subcontinent, and East Pakistan, located in the northeastern corner. The result of the partition was a tragic loss of millions of lives, displacement of millions of refugees, and the 1947 India-Pakistan war over Kashmir, which has provided the basis for more violent conflicts and war between India and Pakistan.

Despite the travails of the new state and the common suffering of both Muslims and Hindus, Pakistan emerged with great promise. Its leaders thought of it as a modernist and democratic model for other Muslim countries, with secular courts, schools, and other institutions. Mohammad Ali Jinnah, the founding father of Pakistan, speaking as Governor-General, told Pakistan's first Constituent Assembly in 1947: "Now, if we want to make this great State of

Pakistan happy and prosperous we should wholly and solely concentrate on the well-being of the people, and especially of the masses and the poor. If you will work in co-operation, forgetting the past, burying the hatchet, you are bound to succeed." [8]

A subsequent war with India in 1965 did not resolve the territorial dispute over Kashmir, and the 1971 war over East Pakistan led to that region's independence as Bangladesh. Islam once again proved not strong enough to hold together this Muslim realm, separated as it was not only by geography, but also by regional, ethnic, and cultural interests.

The 1970s: War, Revolution, and Division

During Europe's colonial dominance in Muslim realms, the blame for the lack of economic and social justice—not to mention democracy—could be left at the door of the colonial powers. Following the end of colonial rule, delayed progress in the Middle East was rationalized by the unfolding of the protracted Israeli-Palestinian conflict. But that could not explain the lack of social progress in other Muslim societies, including those in North Africa, Iran, Indonesia, Malaysia, and even Pakistan.

Great wealth from oil created another source of bitter contention between Muslim nations—for example, oil-rich Saudi Arabia today has almost four times the per capita income of Jordan. The oil wealth ignited a debate about whether natural resources belong to the entire umma or only to local populations, states, and their rulers.

In the 1970s, three episodes changed the entire political scene in the Middle East and in South Asia.

After East Pakistan broke away and became Bangladesh, Pakistani strategists faced the grim prospect of their shrinking country being squeezed by a hostile India, and later in the 1970s by an expansionist, Soviet-backed regime in Afghanistan. The insecurity of this very young state reached alarming heights. Zulfikar Ali Bhutto, Pakistan's president from 1971 to 1973, had begun a process of Islamizing the secular state's institutions in order to consolidate his political base. Dangerously, he also initiated steps to develop nuclear weapons, following India's lead taken in 1968.[9] "There was a Christian bomb, a Jewish bomb, and now a Hindu bomb. Why not an Islamic bomb?" Bhutto asked.[10] The prospect of an "Islamic bomb" thrilled Islamist militant movements and confirmed the worst suspicions held by some in the West.

Under President Mohammad Zia ul-Haq, who succeeded Bhutto (and had him executed in 1979), the process of Islamization and nuclear weapons development continued. With some success, Zia neutralized American criticism of his nuclear program by citing the 1979 Soviet invasion of Afghanistan and a need to contain the influence of the 1978–79 Islamic revolution in Iran. In these efforts, Zia enlisted the help of the Saudis, Wahhabis, and Americans.[11]

One should not forget that Bhutto's and Zia's dream of an "Islamic bomb" was not confined to Pakistan. Muslim intellectuals, such as Ali A. Mazrui, noted the magnitude of the danger posed by Muslim countries desperate to win major concessions from, *in their view*, an uncompromising Israel and an unsympathetic West. "Islam in despair could be pushed to nuclear terrorism as a version of the Jihad," Mazrui wrote.[12] Pakistan tested a nuclear weapon in 1998, and by some estimates there may be a total of more than 100 nuclear weapons in India and Pakistan today. Along the way, the issue became whether the purpose of Pakistan's nuclear arsenal was to even the balance of power with India or to create an "Islamic bomb," to be used for Islamist causes and for "rectifying" injustices faced by Muslims everywhere.

In Iran, Muslims' pent-up frustrations exploded in 1978 in a revolution led by the ulama, which in turn reverberated in many Muslim nations. Led by Ayatullah Ruhollah Khomeini, the Iranian revolution replaced the pro-Western monarchy with an Islamic republic in 1979. On November 4 of that year, after Khomeini had stirred up anti-Americanism, Iranian students and militants invaded the U.S. Embassy in Tehran and held seventy Americans as hostages for 444 days. The revolution, the ensuing hostage crisis, and America's inability to rescue the hostages, all strengthened the prestige of Ayatullah Khomeini.[13] It was Khomeini who blamed America for threatening the umma with materialism and cultural temptations, and it was Khomeini who called for a holy war against "the Great Satan," the term he coined for the United States.[14]

On the one hand, the revolution became a source of inspiration to other militant Islamists, who saw that a resurgent Islam could "defeat" the United States, displace a U.S.-backed secular ruler, and usher in a model for a religious state. On the other hand, conservative Muslim states and their rulers saw the revolution as a threat—not a religious threat, but a political threat that could create all kinds of new alliances, conflicts, and even wars within the Middle East. In the West, many encouraged these conservative states to contain the Khomeini revolution and indeed welcomed

Iraqi opposition to Iran as a barrier to the expansion of the Iranian revolution. For if the revolution had been successfully exported to other Muslim countries, it would have lent geopolitical credence to the possibility of an Islamist threat to the West and its dependence on Middle East oil.

Recall that Khomeini fomented revolution and sharply criticized "decadent and corrupt" secular governments in Muslim countries. Bemoaning secularization, he once said: "Unfortunately, we have lost Islam. They have completely separated it from politics. They cut off its head and gave the rest to us. . . . As long as Muslims remain in this situation, they cannot reach their glory. The glory of Islam is that which existed at the beginning of Islam." Referring to early Muslims and his view of Islam's continuing mission, Khomeini said, "They destroyed two empires with their few numbers because they wanted to build human beings. Islam does not conquer. Islam wants all countries to become Muslim, of themselves. That is, Islam seeks to make those people who are not human beings, human. . . . Islam exists to correct society, and if a sword is unsheathed, it is unsheathed to destroy the corruptors who do not allow society to be corrected." [15]

The third landmark event of the 1970s, coming on the heels of the Iranian revolution, was the Soviet invasion of Afghanistan in 1979. It provided yet another opportunity for militant Islamists, conservative Muslim states, and the United States to form an alliance of convenience against the Soviets. The invasion was all the more offensive to Islamists because Afghanistan, by having defeated the British empire in three wars, was one of only a handful of Muslim countries that had remained independent in the age of imperialism. The United States, through its allies in the Gulf and Pakistan, provided money, logistical support, and highly sophisticated weapons to *mujahedin*, "holy warriors," from many Muslim societies. Thus the United States helped create what may have been the first Muslim legion to fight against the "infidel" and imperialist Soviet Union. This U.S. policy also strengthened the position of Pakistan as a base of operations and training ground for militant Islamists. In doing so, of course, the United States greatly strengthened Islamist militancy movements, including the Taliban.

A common lesson from these three situations in the 1970s is that the internal tensions and geopolitical interests of Muslim nations defied external efforts to impose any scheme of unity. Even the temporary alliance against the Soviets left a bitter legacy that included twenty years of civil war between Muslims in Afghanistan.

Religious Revivals

Along with these developments, there was an ongoing struggle among groups of Muslim traditionalists. There were religious revivalists, who sought to revive a strict practice of Islam to bring about moral reform. Other traditionalists (discussed in chapter 4) wanted to revive Islam both as a religion and as an ideology—this "political Islam" is termed *Islamism*, and its adherents, *Islamists*.

Islam's religious revivalists, much like fundamentalists in other religious revivals worldwide, often express alienation and anger about the "ravages" of secularism, perceived amorality, and the loss of "traditional values" in the modern world. To this list,

Religious Revivalism Today

The contemporary religious revival era began, some say, with concurrent fundamentalist movements in the United States and elsewhere.[1] As the United States has become more secular, the growth in membership of major religions has been disproportionately among fundamentalist Protestants, conservative Catholics, and Orthodox Jews. So it is not surprising, as Michael Lind notes, that both Democratic and Republican candidates in the 2000 presidential election were evangelical Protestants (not fundamentalists) and both said they had "found Jesus."[2] Similarly, the Democratic vice presidential candidate was an Orthodox Jew, who once said that nonbelievers could not be good citizens. "By the 1990s, right-wing Protestants, Catholics and Jews were setting aside their differences to wage political war on secularism and humanism," which Lind defines as a tradition in which humanists seek guidance in knowledge, history, and science, not supernatural religion, to resolve social problems. He continues, "The extension of the political alliance of 'people of faith' to reactionary Muslims, who share their opposition to feminism, gay rights, abortion, contraception, and freedom from censorship, is the logical next step. . . . Both orthodox Christianity and orthodox Islam are intolerant religions which divide humanity into believers and infidels." And both orthodoxies value faith over reason, Lind points out, recalling that Luther once declared, "Reason is the Devil's whore."

1. Karen Armstrong, *Islam: A Short History* (Modern Library, 2000), pp. 164, 165, 166. See also Karen Armstrong, *The Battle for God* (Alfred A. Knopf, 2000).
2. Michael Lind, "Which Civilisation?" *Prospect* (November 2001).

Islamic revivalists add the desire to preserve their traditions and culture by opposing the homogenizing forces of globalization and popular Western culture.

Fundamentalists—whether in the folds of Christianity, Judaism, Islam, or other religions—typically call for returning to the roots of their religions and giving literal interpretations to selected passages of their holy texts and scriptures. By their very nature, fundamentalists and revivalists consider their doctrines to be the truth and superior to all others; hence they reject any ecumenical compromise or tolerance for other religious ideas as an unacceptable form of moral relativism.

Fundamentalists revitalize religions and raise important questions about the legitimacy of secular laws, ethical norms, and economic systems. But they tend to be uncompromising, rigidly doctrinaire, and willing to roll back many of civilization's achievements claimed by others to be progressive, including human rights, freedom of speech, and intellectual freedom.

Much like fundamentalist movements within any religion, Islamic revivals also lack uniformity. Actually, there are a large number of Islamic revivals, reflecting the religion's vast array of denominations, sects, and subsects, as well as specific ethnic and national identities. Islamic revivals, it is generally believed, surged after Israel's 1967 victory. Proponents say revivals are an inherent part of Islam, inspired by the Muslim beliefs that the religious community declines only when it strays from the Sharia (Islamic law) and that the Qur'an provides God's exact instructions for correcting immorality in private and public life. As the twentieth century drew to a close, Islamic revivals had become an international

Poll: Muslims Like Our Culture, Not Our Foreign Policy

Although Islam's revivalists see America's popular culture as a threat to Islamic tradition and law, an international survey indicates that most people in Muslim countries approve of America's cultural exports but disapprove of U.S. foreign policy. In a survey of residents of predominately Muslim Egypt, Kuwait, Lebanon, Saudi Arabia, United Arab Emirates, Indonesia, Iran, and Pakistan, and for comparison, France and Venezuela in March and April 2002, Zogby International found high levels of approval for American culture, science, and technology.[1] In Iran, for example, 75 percent of those surveyed said they liked to watch American movies, while the French were the least likely to say they liked Hollywood. Interestingly, younger Arabs, as well as Muslims and Arabs who use the Internet, had a more favorable view of the United States than did their elders and non-Internet users.

Yet very few of those polled said they approved of U.S. policy toward Palestine: 1 percent of Kuwaitis, 2 percent of Lebanese, 3 percent of Egyptians and Iranians, 5 percent of Saudis and Indonesians, and 9 percent of Pakistanis. Support in France was not much higher: 12 percent.

"It's not our people or values or culture Arabs [and Muslims] don't like. It's U.S. policy," James Zogby told reporters. "And it's not our movies and satellite TV that hurt America; those are helping us."

1. See www.zogby.com for reports.

phenomenon, growing from grassroots movements into the mainstream of society—reaching the rich, poor, educated, and illiterate alike. Illustrative of the depth of interest in Islamic revivals, an estimated two-thirds of all doctoral candidates in Saudi Arabia are now in Islamic studies.[16]

As noted above, Islamic revivalism differs from the political movement known as Islamism. While revivalists see religious reform as an end in itself, Islamists see Islamic revival as a means to a political goal, namely, the reorganization of the state—by peaceful or violent means, depending on whether they are moderate or militant.

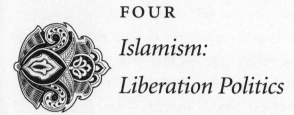

FOUR

Islamism:
Liberation Politics

$\mathcal{I}$SLAMISM IS ANYTHING but a unified movement; Islamist views range across the entire spectrums of both religious and political thought. Jillian Schwedler describes this well:

> Islamism is not a single idea; it has been articulated in response to historical phenomena as diverse as colonialism, new forms of migration, the creation of nation-states, the suppression of labor, leftist mobilization and Western political and economic hegemony. . . . Islamists may be divided into radical and moderate camps, the former aiming to create an Islamic state through revolution and the latter willing to pursue their political agendas within existing (and often quasi-democratic) state institutions. . . . only a tiny percentage of Muslims engage in political projects that can properly be called Islamist. Far more identify with ideologies that are distinctly nationalist, socialist, communist, or democratic.[1]

Islamism, in effect, represents another political promise for the "liberation" of Muslim societies, joining other mass political movements that have evolved over the years.

As discussed above, the first hope was that secular nationalism would liberate Muslims. But while independence fulfilled political aspirations, it did not deliver social justice or modernization or usher in free democracies. Islamists say that nationalism sowed the seeds of disunity and conflict among Muslims by stressing the character and destiny of each Muslim society—instead of promoting a supranational Islamic unity.

During the colonial and postcolonial periods, as well as during the cold war, socialism and Marxism were heralded as the only sure way to achieve these societal goals. But Islamists pointed out that local adaptations of socialism in Libya, Iraq, Syria, Egypt, and elsewhere failed to fulfill their agendas. Islamists see socialism as secular and materialistic, encouraging class warfare and the devaluation of Islam's traditions and ethical values. As an example, they cite the fate of Muslims under oppressive Soviet rule.

After the demise of the Soviet Union, capitalism and the development of free markets in Eastern Europe and in Muslim societies was hailed as the next best way to bring about socioeconomic justice and democracy. Of course, free markets were no panacea. Islamists say that capitalism merely broadens the gap between rich and poor, disrupts traditional patterns of life, and prompts a departure from Islamic history and values.

As to democracy, Islamists cite its contradictions and the gap between theory and practice, especially in Algeria and Turkey. When election results favored the status quo, the elections were considered valid; when an Islamist party won, the results were nullified. Such violations of the spirit of electoral democracy, along with other arbitrary practices, have given Islamists grounds to denounce secular democracy, unregulated markets, and materialism as utter failures or unsuitable to their societies' values.

Islamists consider secularism to be a political and social failure. They advocate placing politics under the aegis of religion—by replacing secular nationalist governments, as well as their laws and institutions, with Islamic ones. In this connection, Islamists have mobilized public opinion and pressured some secular governments—including those of Nigeria, Libya, Sudan, and Pakistan—to start replacing secular laws with Sharia (Islamic law), which regulates everything from banking rules to school curriculums. As Muslim countries reintroduce Sharia, the Islamists hope that secular differences among states will begin to evaporate—and that Islamic law will eventually bring about a common ground and an international Muslim unity as well.

Moderates and Militants

Islamists advance not one, but many kinds of idealistic, moderate, and extremist ideas. Moderate Islamists, for example, want a transcendent Muslim umma—confusing Muslim solidarity with Muslim unity on all issues. Such unity could not be achieved in the early centuries of Islam; today it will be even more difficult to transcend all differences in class, race, ethnicity, culture, region, and national identity. After all, although some of the boundaries of Muslim states were artificially imposed by colonial powers, these borders have created their own reality after fifty years. And the fact is that since 1979, not a single Muslim state has followed Iran's revolutionary model.

Islamist extremists, for their part, have their own international agendas. Unable to unify any established Muslim state (excluding Afghanistan under the Taliban's brief rule) behind their militant cause, they have attempted to form a confederacy of the like-minded in many Muslim countries and Muslim communities. These extremists see themselves as responsible to no state, not even to the ulama, and they act as freelance warriors in the name of Islam. They hope to promote their movements by winning sympathy and support in Muslim realms, championing and occasionally fighting for popular Muslim causes in Palestine, Kashmir, Bosnia, Kosovo, Chechnya, Nagorno-Karabagh, and elsewhere. Some of these militant Islamists have similarities—including the transparent futility of their goals—with nineteenth century anarchists, who hoped their terrorism and assassinations would start a movement to overthrow all governments, which, by definition, were oppressive.

While they advocate universal goals, militant Islamists in the meantime have had some limited successes in pursuing narrowly focused goals within their own societies. The Islamic Salvation Front won elections in Algeria, but their victories were undemocratically nullified by the military.[2] In Muslim realms that have been jolted by population explosion and mass migration to urban centers, Islamism has been presented as a viable alternative to ineffective governments for the provision of economic and social justice.[3]

THE MUSLIM BROTHERHOOD

Currently, one of the most prominent Islamist groups is the Ikhwān al Muslimūn, the Muslim Brotherhood. It is reputed to be the Middle East's largest social movement, combining religious piety with political advocacy, along with the provision of a vast array of nonprofit services, including health clinics, hospitals, factories, schools, youth programs, and adult education.[4] The organization's membership includes a cross-section of Muslim society, including well-educated, middle-class moderates. Its leaders are sharply critical of Western imperialism and capitalism as well as corrupt Muslim governments, but they work within the system and participate in electoral politics. One recent election slogan, "Islam is the solution," sums up the group's belief that social justice and economic improvement will require a social revolution based on an Islamic revival.[5]

Founded in 1928 in Egypt by Hassan al-Banna, the Brotherhood began with his aggressive message: "It is the nature of Islam to dominate, not to be dominated, to impose its laws on all nations and to extend its power to the entire planet." Even though the Brotherhood denied, and continues to deny, any involvement in terrorism or subversion, an attempted assassination of Egyptian president Gamal Abdel Nasser was attributed to the organization, and Nasser subsequently jailed its leaders and banned it as a political party in 1954. Its members have gotten around the ban by campaigning in elections as independents, however, and the organization has continued to grow in Egypt and has also formed branches in other Muslim countries.[6]

One of the leaders jailed in 1954 was Sayyid Qutb, who is considered the father of modern militant Islamism. Curiously enough, he was radicalized by a trip he took to the United States in 1948–49 as an official in the Egyptian Ministry of Education, to learn about the U.S. education system. He was infuriated by anti-Arab prejudice, but he was also shocked by women's freedom and by church services—which he described as "entertainment centers and sexual playgrounds." When he returned to Egypt, he joined the Muslim Brotherhood.

For Qutb, "Islam and the West were incompatible, two camps between which coexistence was impossible. There could only be a struggle between believers and non-believers, between secularism, capitalism, and Islam. Modernization to him was the triumph of the West and the defeat of Islam. . . . He thought that the West, with its emphasis on science and technology, was obliterating the validity of religion."[7] Qutb predicted the death of capitalism and criticized all attempts to reconcile Islam with contemporary society.

A prolific and best-selling writer, Qutb became a persuasive advocate for jihad, or holy war, as he used Islamic history to develop rationales for Muslims to overthrow governments they considered to be corrupt, Westernized, or in violation of Islamic law. His main concern was the "welfare" of Muslim countries, but he also wrote polemics against Christians, Jews, and "Western ways."[8] Qutb spent ten or eleven years in prison (where he completed a thirty-volume commentary on the Qur'an entitled *Fi Zalal al-Qur'an* (In the Shadow of the Qur'an) and ultimately was hanged in 1966, at the age of sixty. His militant Islamist views, however, influenced an entire generation of militants, including the Taliban and al-Qaida.[9]

Today, while the Muslim Brotherhood officially opposes terrorism, it calls openly for armed confrontation against Israel on behalf of the Palestinians. The Brotherhood has been linked to the emergence of some extremist organizations, such as Hamas and Islamic Jihad.[10]

THE TALIBAN

The Taliban's brand of jihadic Islamism called on Islamists from around the world to create an Islamic state based on the most puritanical and extremist reading of the Qur'an by leaders who had received only an elementary religious education.[11] They gained control of most of Afghanistan in 1996, using religious discipline, tribal support, logistical and military aid from Pakistan, and financial support from Saudi Arabia and the Gulf states. Even the United States welcomed the Taliban as a stabilizing force, only to be disappointed by their excesses and lack of any plan for strengthening the economy or establishing a representative government—not to mention that they allowed Afghanistan to become a haven for al-Qaida. The Taliban used sophisticated weapons and communications equipment—some of it left over from the U.S.-backed fight against the Soviet Union—but otherwise their outlook was starkly antimodern.

The Taliban hung televisions from trees. They banned music, picnics, wedding parties, pet birds, paper bags, the wearing of white socks, the shaving of beards, magazines, newspapers, most books, and children's toys. They closed schools for girls and banned women from working outside the home. They cut off women's thumbs for wearing nail polish.[12] They executed Muslims who left "the faith," including members of the Shii denomination called *Hazaras*. UNICEF reported that half of all Afghan children had personally witnessed torture.[13] This "human rights catastrophe," as Amnesty International called it, was carried out in the name of purifying Islam as a theocracy.[14]

But even before September 11, 2001, the Taliban had been rejected as extremist by mainstream Muslim nations. In 1998 Iran even threatened to invade Afghanistan and eliminate the Taliban because they had persecuted Shii citizens and killed Iranian diplomats, but international pressure, including from the United States, prevented it.[15] Of the fifty-six member nations in the Organization of the Islamic Conference, only three recognized the Taliban— Pakistan, Saudi Arabia, and United Arab Emirates—and by November 2001, none did.[16]

ISLAMIC PARTIES

For many people, especially Westerners, it is often difficult to distinguish between activist Islamist parties, which promote Islam as an ideology in a theocratic state, and Islamic parties, whose traditionalist members want secular political systems to reflect the moral principles of their religion. In Indonesia in 1999, for example, Abd al-Rahman Wahid, the leader of one of the world's largest Islamic organizations, Nahdatul Ulama, won the elections that followed the demise of General Suharto's military regime. By comparison, an Islamist party that campaigned on replacing secular laws with Sharia won only 1.7 percent of the vote.[17] Wahid subsequently left office according to the democratic process in 2001.[18] Nahdatul Ulama, founded in 1926, and Muhammadiyah, founded in 1912, are Indonesia's mainstream parties, with a combined membership of between 60 million and 80 million. Since

September 11, these two relatively tolerant and liberal parties have been working together to refute the messages of Islamist groups, including Laskar Jihad and its few thousand members.[19]

A Faltering Mass Movement?

As a mass movement, Islamism has struggled with its many competing constituencies and agendas. Starting in the mid- to late twentieth century, according to Gilles Kepel, Islamism grew with support from three critical constituencies: intellectuals who promoted an Islamist theocracy, devout middle-class professionals who had fared poorly in the postcolonial period and wanted a greater voice in an Islamist government, and large numbers of disgruntled, rebellious urban youths who saw secular regimes as hopelessly corrupt and unsalvageable.[20]

Islamism's greatest success was Ayatullah Khomeini's revolution in Iran. Islamist movements gained international momentum as Iran attempted to export its revolution to other Muslim societies. The leading conservative force against the spread of the revolution was Saudi Arabia's ruling dynasty and the orthodox Wahhabi ulama. These Sunni Muslims could not afford to see a Shii model gain momentum as *the* model for an Islamic state. As a result, the Saudis began exporting their own model, which combined a secular monarchy with puritanical Wahhabism—along with generous financial aid for Islamist organizations, religious schools, and social services in Pakistan, Central Asia, and elsewhere. The Saudi strategy had the benefit of winning public support at home, in other secular Muslim nations, and even in the United States—while at the same time encouraging Islamists to exhaust their energy for militant campaigns outside the Saudi kingdom.

The rivalry between Iran and Saudi Arabia kept these two distinct Islamist movements alive, and during the 1980s they joined together in a jihad against the Soviets in Afghanistan. After the Soviet defeat, though, the Islamist movement fractured, as its constituencies split because of inherent disagreements over goals and strategies: the youthful and battle-hardened mujahedin, "holy warriors," wanted to use violence to replace corrupt systems with Islamic states, while the middle classes wanted to peacefully "paint the system green" (Kepel refers to the Islamic symbolism of green as the color of the Prophet Muhammad's flag). In Kepel's assessment, Islamism declined as a mass political movement as violence and terrorism spread around the world, as the Taliban regime in Afghanistan and another Islamist regime in Sudan evolved into military dictatorships, and as Iran's electorate asserted its will by voting in moderate leaders to ease rigid religious rules and promote liberal democratic processes. Between 1995 and 1997 the "high season of jihad" was drawing to a close in many Muslim countries. To Kepel, the terrorist attacks on September 11, 2001, represented not a growing threat from Islamism but the reverse: they were a symbol of its "isolation, fragmentation and decline." He acknowledges that Islamist terrorism still poses a threat, but he predicts that without public support, this form of extremism will ultimately fade away. It is an optimistic view, but one hopes his analysis is correct.[21]

STATELESS TERRORISTS JOIN IN ABUSE OF RELIGION

In the midst of these competing mass movements, there has grown up a third kind of militant Islamism, one that does not need a mass

Accountability to God—and the People

Islamist political systems set themselves very difficult standards to meet. "The basic tenet of Islamism—that government should be accountable to God's rules—may ultimately prove the movement's greatest weakness," writes Max Rodenbeck. "It is easy enough to point out other people's infringements of those rules. It is a far more difficult thing to observe them, all the time, yourself. Unless of course, it is you who defines the rules—but the history of Islam shows that no one since the time of the Prophet has been able to monopolize the interpretation of the scriptures that contain *shari'a's* rules. The cry that is so often directed by Islamists at governments—'Your way is not the way of Islam'—can be and is indeed raised by rival movements against each other. So has it been for fourteen centuries and so, doubtless, will it continue to be. And yet the practical message implied by today's Islamist challenge, which is that governments in most Muslim countries are not accountable enough to anyone, is well worth considering. These are governments which, in the words of Nazih Ayubi, tend to combine omnipotence with incompetence. In seeking to make them accountable to God, Islamism has also pushed them to be more accountable to their people."[1]

1. Max Rodenbeck, "Is Islamism Losing Its Thunder?" *Washington Quarterly,* vol. 21, no. 2 (Spring 1998), p. 177.

movement to accomplish its goals. These are Islamists who have no return addresses. They have emerged when the vulnerabilities of our global societies and sophisticated technologies can be used to wreak havoc for specific, general, or sometimes even unspecified goals of a religious nature. Although their tactics may be new, their use of religion as an ideological weapon is not new, nor is it likely to go away. Even Lenin attempted to use Islam as a vehicle for what was called the "national liberation" of the peoples of the East in 1919–20. During the cold war, the United States and other Western countries used Islam to contain communism. Iran and other Muslim nations have used Islam to promote capitalism and defend private property, with the ulama and politicians pointing out that the Prophet Muhammad was a merchant. Islam has also been used to support socialism and dictatorships—to the extent that during the Persian Gulf war in 1991 the secular, socialist party of Saddam Hussein added the words *Allahu Akbar* (God is great) to the Iraqi flag.[22] Later, in the mid-1990s, Saddam Hussein banned the serving of alcohol in public places and established a radio station dedicated to religious programs.[23] So it is not surprising that now there are many individuals and groups, both secular and Islamist, attempting to use Islam as a mobilizing tool as well as a vehicle for their particular political ideologies, beliefs, or interests—however far-fetched they may be.

Strategies for Promoting Islamism

Parties that exploit Islam receive a wide audience largely because there are so many unresolved political issues left over from the postcolonial and postcommunist eras. Following the demise of the Soviet Union—and 150 years of Russian and Soviet efforts to dominate, marginalize, and even eliminate Islam—Islamists found a great opportunity to fill the power vacuum in the Central Asian republics.[24] Likewise, there was a widespread sense of outrage over the treatment of Muslims in Kashmir, Palestine, Chechnya, Bosnia, and Kosovo. So it is that some militant Islamists say, essentially: God has given us many people, wealth, and intelligence. We need to organize ourselves into a great force, equipped with nuclear weapons, because that is the only way the geopolitical powers will help rectify "historical injustices."

It is not surprising, therefore, that moderate and militant Islamists have seized on some major issues to galvanize support:

—The fifty-year saga of the Palestinian conflict, including the Israeli occupation of the West Bank and the Gaza Strip and the plight of the refugees, has provided Islamists with a compelling narrative to win the sympathy of Muslims worldwide. Islamists have used that public sympathy to undermine secular Arab regimes, which are blamed for their inability to resolve the Palestine issue by defeating or containing Israel. Islamists also exploit the plight of Palestinians as a way to destroy confidence in the United Nations and the major powers, accusing them all of being unable or unwilling to enforce various UN resolutions pertaining to the conflict and the creation of a Palestinian state.

—Kashmir, also a blood-splattered half-century-old issue, has given Islamists yet another tragic situation to exploit. They point to the "mistreatment" of Muslims and the inability of the UN and geopolitical powers to respond to the "legitimate aspirations of the people of Kashmir" by granting them the right of self-determination.

—In addition, the presence of "infidels" on the Arabian peninsula is a very sore point for many Islamists. They frequently portray the U.S. military presence as an insulting, aggressive intrusion on the umma near the very home of the Prophet and holy cities of Islam.

Martyrs for the Cause?

Amir Taheri, author of *The Cauldron: Middle East behind the Headlines,* has described the religious problem with promoting suicide bombers as Muslim martyrs, noting that Islam expressly forbids suicide as an "unpardonable sin," along with cannibalism, murder, incest, and rape.[1] As a result, the "apologists of terror" have stopped using the word *entehari*, meaning "suicidal," and have coined the term *etsesh'had*, which literally means "affidavit," to convey the idea of "martyrlike." They do not use *shahid*, the word for "martyr" or "witness," as it is imbued with religious meanings. Allah, after all, is considered the First Witness, and in Islamic history only a dozen or so Muslims have been considered shahid for having fallen in battle while defending the faith. For suicide bombing to be formally accepted in Islam, Taheri says, the practice would have to be defined, given rules, justified by Islamic law, and then approved by a consensus among Muslim communities—"something the prophets of terror will never secure." Yet this has not stopped many Muslim politicians: "Foreign ministers from 57 Muslim

Islamists dismiss or ignore all efforts by the United States and other Western nations to protect Muslim and human rights.[25] Actually, Islamists argue that the "continuing horror" in both Palestine and Kashmir is due to an anti-Muslim "conspiracy" between geopolitical powers and some of their "client" states—including not only Israel and India, but also pro-Western Arab and Muslim states. It is this "collusion," Islamists say, that prevents a "just resolution" of these festering issues. And in an extraordi-

countries met in Kuala Lumpur, Malaysia . . . with the stated intention of defining terrorism and distancing Islam from terror. Instead, they ended up endorsing the suicide bombers."

Also worth noting is Shibley Telhami's observation that for Palestinians, suicide bombing has gone beyond its religious justification to become a secular tactic as well. "From nonreligious young women to members of the semi-Marxist Popular Front for the Liberation of Palestine to the secular Al Aksa Martyrs Brigades, groups and individuals have begun emulating the suicides of Hamas, the radical Islamist group. . . . Like all terrorism, suicide bombings must be delegitimized by Arab societies and stopped because no ends can justify these horrific means. At the same time, there has to be a way of dealing with the realities that have made suicide bombings acceptable to a large number of Palestinians and others."[2]

1. Amir Taheri, "The Semantics of Murder," *Wall Street Journal,* May 8, 2002. See also Amir Taheri, *The Cauldron: The Middle East behind the Headlines* (London: Hutchinson, 1988).

2. Shibley Telhami, "Why Suicide Terrorism Takes Root," *New York Times,* April 4, 2002, p. A23. See also Ruthven, *A Fury for God.*

nary abuse of Islam, militant Islamists, and non-Islamists as well, have promoted suicide bombing as a form of martyrdom.

Islamists are not alone in exploiting the Palestinian and Kashmiri issues. Various regimes in the Middle East and South Asia have used these hostilities as justification for vast military expenditures—citing the heightened requirement for self-defense or even the possibility of needing to confront Israel, Pakistan, or India. And some political parties and regimes have used these issues to rationalize a military buildup that strengthens their hold on political power—and to deflect attention from their failure to address the socioeconomic needs of their people.

Clearly, a just resolution of the issues in Palestine—and an international order guaranteeing it—is crucial for the stability of the Middle East and the long-term safety of Israel. As President George W. Bush noted recently, "It is untenable for Israeli citizens to live in terror. It is untenable for Palestinians to live in squalor and occupation. . . . Permanent occupation threatens Israel's identity and democracy. A stable, peaceful Palestinian state is necessary to achieve the security that Israel longs for."[26] Many people, even in Israel, have called for a Palestinian state, but several questions remain unanswered, including what kind of state and government structure the Palestinians want.[27] Kashmir is another powder keg, and resolution of the dispute is critically needed to prevent a nuclear war between Pakistan and India. With these issues resolved, and thus the removal of excuses for excessive military budgets, ruling regimes will have to address long-neglected domestic priorities—or face the consequences of political upheaval.

That said, while the resolution of these issues would bring peace and stability, it would not immediately solve enormous domestic problems. Indeed, it would initially focus public attention on the need to deal with internal factors, including corruption, misrule, endemic inequalities, lack of political participation, and inadequate health, education, and welfare systems. Nor would peace in Palestine and Kashmir solve other inter-Muslim tensions and conflicts over irredentist ethnic and nationalist movements or disputes about borders and resources such as oil and water.

Nor, of course, will all the militant Islamists pack their bags and retire. After all, radical ideologies do not always spring from poverty and despair; on the contrary, they attract individuals who often have relatively good education and incomes.[28] Though their numbers would be diminished as they lost public support, some extremists would certainly look for other issues to stir up and exploit as they continued to dream about creating some great militant Islamic state that would unite the entire umma.

FIVE

Quests for Democracy and Modernity

ONE OF THE BIGGEST challenges for moderate Islamists seems to be figuring out how to adapt the principles of democracy to their cultures and traditions. As John Esposito and John Voll write, "Religious resurgence and democratization [were] two of the most important developments of the final decades of the twentieth century." Moreover, "the demand for democracy, the growth of prodemocracy movements, is now evident throughout much of the Muslim world."[1] Why, then, has the process of democratization and modernization been so slow, or in some places nonexistent? Shireen T. Hunter summarizes the debate taking place both in Western and Muslim societies:

Some believe that because of its fusion of temporal and spiritual realms, Islam is incompatible with modernity and democracy. This group also notes that all religious systems that put divinely inspired law and ethics above those developed by

humans are intrinsically incompatible with rationalist thinking, and thus also with modernity and democratization.

Others note that in reality there was a much clearer distinc-
tion between politics and religion in the Muslim world than
that which existed in Christendom until the advent of the Age
of Reason. The question is whether Islam is any more dogmatic
than other religions. The first group believes the answer to this
question is yes, while the latter maintains that the answer is no.

An impartial reading of the history of both the Muslim
world and the West shows that the processes of modernization
and democratization have more to do with stages of economic
change and their social and cultural consequences than with
peculiarities of different religions. . . . Nevertheless, literalist
and reductionist interpretations of key Islamic injunctions have
been used by some Muslims to prevent the advancement of
both processes. The challenge is to encourage the more progressive and liberal trends within Islam in order to help in the
Muslim world's move toward modernization and democracy.[2]

Recalling some of the historical context for this debate,
Abdullahi Ahmed An-Na'im, a political dissident from the Sudan
who now teaches at Emory School of Law, notes that nineteenth-
and twentieth-century politics, not religion, largely explains the
slow pace of modernization and democratization:

Every Muslim country today was either colonized by the West
or subjected to tremendous Western control. Colonialism was
not in the business of promoting democratic values or institu-

tions. And after independence, you get oppressive regimes that
are supported by Western powers for strategic interests. So people never had a chance to develop these values and processes.
. . . Post-colonialism, not Islam, is what's really at issue here.
Islam just happens to be the religion of a people who have been
denied the possibility of experimenting and learning.[3]

Today, there is much experimenting and learning taking place
in many Muslim societies. And, of course, discussion about
whether democracy is appropriate is not confined to Muslim
nations; in the past similar questions have been raised about
Russian and Chinese societies and whether they are ready for
"Western" style democracy. Even the nature of democracy is subject to debate, for there is no single, universally accepted, operating model of democracy. Nor are Western democracies free from
intolerance. But the generally accepted principles of democracy,
including those among most Muslim societies, include representative government, free political parties, free elections, a free press,
the protection of minorities, a balance of power among the exec-
utive, independent judiciary, and legislative branches of government—and above all, the rule of law.

Democracy is not a total stranger to Muslim societies—and in
some ways, they have been leaders. For while the Taliban refused to
allow women even to leave their homes unaccompanied, never
mind giving them the right to vote—next door in Pakistan, women
not only had the right to vote but could be elected to high office.
During the last twenty years, women have held the highest elected
offices in Pakistan, Bangladesh, Turkey, and Indonesia.[4] But even in

Democracy in the Muslim World

Westerners tend to hear a disproportionate amount about the Persian Gulf's emirs, sheikhs, and sultans, but there is a wide variety of political systems operating in Muslim nations. In addition to democracies in Bangladesh, Turkey, and Senegal, there are emerging democracies in Albania and Indonesia. There are also other complex political systems: authoritarian states with democratic elements in Algeria, Egypt, and Azerbaijan; authoritarian regimes in Iraq, Syria, and Libya; monarchies in Bahrain, Saudi Arabia, and United Arab Emirates; monarchies with some democratic elements in Jordan, Malaysia, and Morocco; a theocracy with democratic elements in Iran; and finally, systems in flux, such as in Nigeria, which shifted from military to civilian rule, and Pakistan, where the military has suspended democracy.[1]

1. See *CIA World Factbook* (2001) and U.S. State Department, as cited in "A Spectrum of Governments in the Islamic World," *New York Times*, November 23, 2001.

these enlightened states, female leaders like Indonesia's current president, Megawati Sukarnoputri, often face intense criticism from conservative political and religious leaders.[5]

In the Muslim debate, modernists and traditionalists have very different ideas about democracy. Some traditionalists see no separation, in principle, between state and religion, with God being the sovereign authority, not the people. Other Muslim scholars and rulers—especially the monarchs and dictators—have often rejected Western-style democracy as being too divisive and too centered on the individual and the temporal materialistic world. They cling to the old notion that their authority comes not from the people alone, but also from their historic role as defenders of the Muslim faith and its communities.

Some even welcome Benito Mussolini's notion of a state and its single official party as an "antiparty party"—one party in charge of every aspect of society, including religion. "The Fascist State organizes the nation," Mussolini wrote, "but leaves a sufficient margin of liberty to the individual; the latter is deprived of all useless and possibly harmful freedom, but retains what is essential; the deciding power in this question cannot be the individual, but the State alone."[6]

According to one of the most famous traditional political theorists, Abu al-Ala al-Mawdudi, the ideal Islamic state would be the "kingdom of God," or a theocracy.[7] In this kingdom, "the entire Muslim population runs the state in accordance with the Book of God and the practice of His Prophet. If I were permitted to coin a new term, I would describe this system of government as 'theo-democracy,' that is to say a divine democratic government, because under it the Muslims have been given a limited popular sovereignty under the suzerainty of God."

Modernist scholars, including Rifa'a al-Tahtawi in nineteenth-century Egypt, often believed that Western ideas were compatible with Islam, because they recognized Islam's large contributions to Western civilization. Therefore they placed great emphasis on the exercise of reason and knowledge—in every area, including understanding the Qur'an and the Prophet's sayings and searching the entire history of Islam for insights.

Another important modernist and religious reformer in Egypt was Muhammad Abduh (1849–1905). He, like other scholars around the same time—notably Sayyid Jamal ad-Din al-Afghani in Iran and elsewhere the in Middle East and Sayyid Ahmed Khan and Muhammad Iqbal on the Indian subcontinent—called for reopening the "gates of ijtihad," interpretation of holy texts, as a critical step toward the modernization of Islam. Abduh, who became the Grand Mufti in Egypt in 1889, wrote that the Qur'an was not entirely God's Word, but also included the Prophet Muhammad's own fallible human thinking on the organization of society and its institutions. Thus he argued that one could be both a pious Muslim and a modernist: "The Book gives us all that God permits us, or is essential for us, to know about His attributes. But, it does not require our acceptance of its contents simply on the ground of its own statement of them. On the contrary, it offers arguments and evidence. . . . It spoke to the rational mind and alerted the intelligence." Abduh and his protégé Rashid Rida (1865–1935) published *al-Manar*, a journal that helped to inspire modernist intellectuals from North Africa to Indonesia.[8]

At the start of the twentieth century, Abduh and al-Afghani founded a reform movement called Salafiyyah (from *salaf as-salihiin*, meaning "the pious ancestors") that gained influence in many Muslim realms. Salafiyyah sought modernization within Islamic principles and reason. Interestingly, its followers included Qasim Amin (1863–1908), who wrote two books with feminist themes: *The Emancipation of Women*, and *The New Woman*.[9]

More recently, Mahmoud Mohammad Taha, founder of a prodemocracy movement in Sudan, maintained that there had to be a clear separation between religion and state if religious practice and public discussion were to thrive. He was hanged for heresy in 1985. Abdullahi Ahmed An-Na'im considers Taha a mentor and says, "The [Qur'an] is a powerful sacred text, but we must recognize that our understanding of it is both historically conditioned and shaped by human agency."[10]

There are other Muslim intellectuals who are trying to cope with the major challenges facing Islam, especially as these relate to the interaction between modernity and tradition. For example, Muhammad al-Ghazali, a former member of the Muslim Brotherhood, has come out for selective modernization, especially in regard to science and technological progress, while reserving the right to disagree with some philosophical elements in the West. Perhaps the most impressive Muslim intellectual today is Mohamed Talbi. He believes that balance between faith and reason is possible and inevitable; that faith is the choice of the individual and does not conflict with or constrain reason. "There is," he says, "no meaning to faith if there is no freedom or choice. The renewal of Islam is more to do with questions of the social and political order than with questions of theology which remain entirely sound. Muslims have suffered because they have used Islam politically." Moreover, Talbi considers that all knowledge is provisional, and therefore everyone must live with some degree of uncertainty with respect to their knowledge. Thus he rejects absolutism. Talbi is also an advocate of pluralism and religious tolerance, for man, he says, is by nature a pluralist.[11]

Talbi is not alone in taking up the difficult issues around Islam and modernity. Mohamed Charfi, the former minister of education of Tunisia, has written eloquently on Islam and liberty, Islam and the state, and Islam and the law. Most important of all, however, he has highlighted the urgent and essential need to modernize educational systems in order to ensure the progress of Muslim societies. He stresses that Islam has been misinterpreted, that it is not incompatible with either reason, science, progress, or modernity.[12]

The other outstanding intellectuals who are grappling with the intellectual challenges facing Islamic societies are, interestingly, also North African. One is Mohammed Arkoun, whose works—*Lectures du Coran, Rethinking Islam: Common Questions, Uncommon Answers,* and *La pensée arabe*—have stimulated timely and widespread intellectual dialogue. Abdou Filali-Ansary is equally influential; his works, which include *L'Islam est-il hostile à la laïcité?* and *Par souci de clarté: A propos des sociétés musulmanes contemporaines,* are the subject of international debate.[13]

Another important voice is that of 'Abd al-Karim Soroush, whose writings include *Reason, Freedom, and Democracy in Islam.* He has criticized the "sanctimonious piety" of those who have sought to use religion to assert authoritarian power and "disguise some of their less pious, self-serving economic interests." Soroush points out that while the establishment claims that politics is serving Islam, the reverse is actually true: currently, it is religion that is being manipulated to serve politics. Therefore, many religious interpretations are becoming corrupted by political and economic interests. Soroush also is an uncompromising champion of human rights: "A religion that is oblivious to human rights (including the need for humanity for freedom and justice) is not tenable in the modern world. In other words, religion needs to be right not only logically but also ethically . . . we cannot evade rational, moral and extrareligious principles and reasoning about human rights. . . . A rule that is not just is not religious."[14]

Fatima Mernissi, who teaches sociology at the University of Mohammed V in Rabat, Morocco, has raised fundamental issues about women and Islam, concluding in her book *The Veil and the Male Elite: A Feminist Interpretation of Women's Rights in Islam* that the quest for women's full participation in the political and social affairs of their countries "stems from no imported Western values, but is a true part of the Muslim tradition."[15]

Modernists also maintain that Islam is imbued with ancient traditions that lay the foundation for a secular democracy. These include the principles that Muslims consult others for mutual understanding in making decisions; that they seek consensus through collective judgment (though in practice this has often meant seeking consensus among Islamic scholars); and that as times and circumstances bring new problems, humanity has the God-given rational faculty to find answers by independently consulting the Qur'an and the Prophet's teachings.[16] "The principles of Islam are dynamic, it is our approach which has become static," the reformer Altaf Gauhar has written.[17] In a compromise position, some scholars argue for a gradual introduction of democracy, learning the lessons of the "deficiencies" and "inefficiencies" of Western practice, while also maintaining social stability.

Clearly, the delicate relationship between mosque and state, as well as the principles of Islamic and secular law, will be paramount in all Muslim discussions about democracy. Another democratic necessity is an informed electorate: will Muslim states choose to mandate, and bring into effect, freedom of speech and free education as rights for all? Muslim societies and states face many challenging questions. How can they cope with the principles of democracy, such as voting and the rule of the majority? And if Islamist parties win democratic elections in secular societies, should they be banned, as they have been in Turkey and Algeria? But then, why should members of an Islamist party respect the spirit of democracy, if it does not allow them to win "free" elections? Similarly, how could one guarantee that an Islamist party that came to power would relinquish that power if it was subsequently challenged and defeated at the polls? Do Islamists favor "one person, one vote, one time"?[18]

Time to Deal with Tough Questions

The worldwide challenge, not only for Muslim societies, but for all societies and democracies, is to come to grips with economic justice and freedom, as well as the interplay of modernism and traditionalism, secularism and religion, and individual rights and societal or collective rights. Jalal al-Din Rumi, the thirteenth-century Sufi scholar—and, interestingly, America's best-selling poet today—once wrote: "Start a huge foolish project, like Noah."[19]

For Muslim societies, the immediate challenge is assuming responsibility for modernizing their economies and governing structures. In this connection, General Pervez Musharraf, Pakistan's leader, recently challenged his people to consider fundamental options: "The day of reckoning has come. Do we want Pakistan to become a theocratic state? Do we believe that religious education alone is enough for governance? Or do we want Pakistan to emerge as a progressive and dynamic Islamic welfare

state?" Militant Islamists, he added, "did nothing except contribute to bloodshed in Afghanistan. I ask of them whether they
know anything other than disruption and sowing seeds of hatred.
Does Islam preach this?"[20]

There is a healthy debate in Muslim societies about the proper
role of religion in the state. Questions include: How can Muslim
authorities reconcile the disagreements among secular law, tribal
law, local customs, Islamic law, and international law—does
Islamic law transcend the others or accommodate them? What
place do dogmatic, militant Islamists have in democratic society?
How does Islam discourage or prevent ordinary citizens and
groups from presuming to interpret Islamic law and issuing legal
opinions—and calls for holy war? What is the definition of a
national liberation movement? How is such a movement distinguished from terrorism? What is the position of Islamic societies
on suicide used in the name of either national liberation or terrorism, when Islam, like most religions, condemns suicide as a sin?

It has been said that Muslim leaders' response to the September 11 attacks were "mixed, muddled and muttered."[21] In fact
there been no shortage of individual expressions of outrage—
from many unexpected as well as welcome sources, including
Ayatullah Ali Khameneì, Supreme Jurist-Ruler of Iran, and Sheikh
Abdul-Rahman al-Sudais at the Grand Mosque in Mecca. But
apart from the press releases from established organizations like
the League of Arab States and the Organization of the Islamic
Conference, there have been no collective, substantive, and authoritative responses from religious and political leaders explicitly
defining, condemning, and outlawing terrorism, and setting pun-
ishments for those who wage terrorism. This is, I believe, because

many Muslims are deeply conflicted: they can rationalize and perhaps even support suicide bombing against civilians in Israel as a form of legitimate "resistance" against an occupying force; but ironically, and morally inconsistently, they denounce the suicide attacks in the United States as being "against all human and Islamic norms"—to quote from a statement released by Islamist leaders, including Sheikh Ahmad Yassin, founder of the Islamic Resistance Movement (Hamas), which claims responsibility for many of the suicide bombings in Israel that have indiscriminately murdered more than 250 people of all ages and faiths in streets, strollers, buses, restaurants, dance halls, and grocery stores.[22]

The relationship between religion and civil rights poses troubling and difficult questions for many Muslim societies. Should Muslim leaders support secular constitutions or abandon them in favor of Sharia? If so, what would happen to the sizable non-Muslim minorities who are citizens of nations such as Nigeria? How will they protect the rights of Muslim minorities like the Shii in Saudi Arabia and Afghanistan and the Sunni in Iran—as well as the Christians, Jews, and other religious minorities? Are minorities in Muslim countries to be tolerated only, or given equality? And how should Muslim societies deal with the issue of self-determination movements, such as the Kurds in Turkey?

Are there sufficient favorable conditions, economic pressures, and political will to enable Muslim nations to cooperate in the creation of regional economic unions, much like the European Union, or even a Muslim common market among all Muslim realms? Is the unity of Muslims reflected only in their stance on Jerusalem, or is it confined to the plight of Palestinians, Kashmiris, Chechens, Bosnians, and Kosovars? Can there be a Muslim version of the World Bank that would share the wealth of rich Muslim countries with poor ones in some form of international investment? These are terribly complex questions, with no easy answers.

Another immediate and pressing issue is the status of women. At a time when women are assuming greater roles around the world in general, and in Muslim nations in particular, it is not possible to avoid debate about how to ensure the rights of women. Why do they have fewer rights than men—to travel, to drive, to marry, to divorce, to inherit, to work?[23] (In 2000, women in Khartoum were forbidden to work in many public places, and the next year Sudan's president refused to recognize a UN treaty on women's rights on the grounds that it violated family law under Sharia.)[24] Should women be silenced in public because tradition-alists consider the female voice sexually provocative?[25] Should women be forced to marry their rapists to avoid "disgracing" their families, as they are in parts of Turkey?[26] Should they be denied the vote because Muslim traditionalists claim in some societies that they introduce an "irrational element" in politics—an out-landish claim similar to those that deprived Swiss women of the vote until 1971 (Switzerland was the last Western country to introduce women's suffrage).[27] And yet in some other Muslim countries women can not only vote, but have also been elected to the highest political offices.

There are many issues surrounding traditional Islamic educa-tion systems. Can states provide an adequate secular school sys-tem, or will they relegate education, by default or decree, to the

Islamic Reaction against 9/11

Sheikh Muhammad Hussain Fadlallah, the spiritual leader of the Hezbollah, who was accused by the United States of ordering the truck bomb that killed 241 American servicemen at the U.S. Marines barracks near Beirut airport in 1983, condemned the September 11 attacks as incompatible with Sharia (Islamic law), for the perpetrators—"merely suicides," not martyrs—killed innocent civilians in a distant land where the victims could not be considered aggressive enemies.[1]

Sheikh Mohammed Sayyed al-Tantawi, of Al-Azhar Mosque and University in Cairo: "Attacking innocent people is not courageous; it is stupid and will be punished on the day of judgment."[2]

Ayatullah Ali Khameneì, Supreme Jurist-Ruler of Iran: "Killing of people, in any place and with any kind of weapons, including atomic bombs, long-range missiles, biological or chemical weapons, passenger or war planes, carried out by any organization, country, or individuals, is condemned. . . . It makes no difference whether such massacres happen in Hiroshima, Nagasaki, Qana, Sabra, Shatila, Deir Yassin, Bosnia, Kosovo, Iraq, or in New York and Washington."[3]

President Muhammad Khatami of Iran: "The horrific attacks of September 11, 2001, in the United States were perpetrated by [a] cult of fanatics who had self-mutilated their ears and tongues, and could only communicate with perceived opponents through carnage and devastation."

Abdulaziz bin Abdallah al-Ashaykh, Chief Mufti of Saudi Arabia: "A form of injustice that cannot be tolerated by Islam

... they will invoke the anger of God Almighty and lead to harm and corruption on Earth."

More than forty Muslim scholars and Islamist leaders, including Mustafa Mashhur, of the Muslim Brotherhood in Egypt; Sheikh Ahmad Yassin, founder of the Islamic Resistance Movement (Hamas) in Palestine; Rashid Ghannoushi, president of the Nahda Renaissance Movement in Tunisia; and Fazil Nour, president of PAS (Parti Islam SeMalaysia) in Malaysia, issued a statement saying: "The undersigned, leaders of Islamic movements, are horrified by the events of Tuesday 11 September 2001, in the United States which resulted in massive killing, destruction and attack on innocent lives. . . . We condemn, in the strongest terms, the incidents, which are against all human and Islamic norms."

The League of Arab States condemned the attacks; its secretary general, Amre Moussa, stated: "It is indeed tormenting that any country or people or city anywhere in the world be the scene of such disastrous attacks."

Dr. Abdelouahed Belkeziz, secretary general of the Organization of the Islamic Conference, whose members represent fifty-seven states, condemned the attacks as "brutal acts that ran counter to all covenants, humanitarian values and divine religions foremost among which is Islam."

1. John F. Burns, "Bin Laden Stirs a Struggle among Muslims about the Meaning of Jihad," *New York Times*, January 20, 2002.

2. U.S. State Department, Network of Terrorism (http://usinfo.state.gov/products/pubs/terrornet/print/quotes.htm).

3. This and all subsequent quotes are from University of North Carolina, Statements against Terror (www.unc.edu/~kurzman/terror.htm).

clerical establishment and its schools, the madrasa, with their peculiar and parochial curricula? Should schools teach only religion or should they allow "Western" science to be taught as well? Do Muslim governments have the authority or the political will to stop school systems from using textbooks that teach contempt for non-Muslims?[28] Will they stop religious schools from fostering hostility toward Jews and Christians? [29] (And how should we, in the West, deal with similar instances where Christians are fomenting anti-Muslim and anti-Jewish hatred?)

Why is it permissible to convert Christians to Islam when Muslims are forbidden to convert to Christianity—and are even subjected to the death penalty, in some Muslim nations? In Sudan, where Sharia is in force, anyone—Muslim or non-Muslim—who violates or rejects Islamic law can be punished by amputation, stoning, flogging, and crucifixion, depending on the violation.[30] The question is, how can a religion modernize itself?

In addition, Muslims face a new challenge—in immigrant communities in Europe, Latin America, the United States, and Australia. How should Muslims reconcile their religious commitments with their political commitments to secular systems in their adopted countries? Writing about these issues, Bat Ye'or notes that "problems of integration and cohabitation . . . will arise between Western societies and Muslim immigrant populations, if the latter adhere to a religious legal code which the Western democratic societies reject." [31]

Modernization and globalization raise even more questions about the interplay of religion, culture, economy, education, and technology. Is it possible to modernize without "Westernizing" or "democratizing," as many Muslims wish? Can a society take

Western technology without taking in some Western values? And besides, are "Western" values really Western—or are they universal values similar to those that prevailed in the Golden Age of Islam? Those who believe that societies can modernize without Westernizing betray a certain naivete in this age of the Internet and the information revolution. There is no "safe" modernization, as there can be no "immunization" against ideas. Modernization has always brought unintended consequences.

SIX

Need for Mutual Knowledge and Understanding

WE LIVE IN HISTORIC times, but by and large, Americans are ahistorical, concerned only with the present and often unappreciative of underlying forces that helped create this present—and that will likely influence our future. As George Will has written, "When Americans say of something, 'That's history,' they mean it is irrelevant." [1] Unfortunately, it is not.

Today, one can regret but not be surprised that we as a society know so little about the world, including the actual divisions and affinities of the three Abrahamic faiths. In a 2000 survey, only one in fourteen Americans claimed to really understand Islam's basic tenets; hopefully this ratio has improved since then. [2] But a more recent survey found that one in four high school students was unable even to name the ocean that separates North America from Asia. [3] It is clear, however, that we cannot be ignorant about the history of one-fifth of humanity. Nor can we ignore the common bonds among the three Abrahamic faiths.

A "Clash of Civilizations"?

There are some who say that civilizations, instead of becoming bridges of understanding, become walls of separation, destined to spur clashes. To the questions "Is there a monolithic Islam?" and "If so, does it pose a real threat to the West?" these clash-of-civilization theorists answer yes. Most notable among them is Samuel P. Huntington, who in *The Clash of Civilizations and the Remaking of World Order* and more recent writings follows Arnold Toynbee's scholarship but derives a different conclusion.

Huntington theorizes that with the fall of communism, wars of politics and ideology have yielded to wars between cultures. "Cultural commonalities and differences shape the interests, antagonisms and associations of states," he writes.[4] Forecasting the West's decline, he hypothesizes that Muslim and Asian countries will align themselves against the West, and there will be some "swing" civilizations, including Japan, Russia, and India. A single, virulent Islamism, then, in this theory, replaces communism, producing cold war II. The "Green Menace," we are told, has replaced the "Red Menace."

Huntington and others who write about a clash of civilizations do not recognize that class, tribal, family, personal, ethnic, cultural, economic, and national interests have always defied a unity of purpose that transcends all these divisions. As shown above, instances when the Muslim world was a unified monolith have been extremely rare. Throughout Islamic history, the gravitational pull of regional, dynastic, and since the nineteenth century nationalist interests has consistently outweighed the spiritual affiliations of some idealized, transcendent, organic umma. If history is a guide, it shows that in Islam, as in most major religions, there is a broad gulf between the ideal of unity and the realities on the ground.

Even during the Golden Age of Islam, at the height of the Abbasid empire, there were rival caliphates in Córdoba and in North Africa, as well as ethnically based Turkic and Iranian dynasties that challenged Baghdad's authority and at times reduced the Abbasid Caliph to a mere figurehead. Subsequently, there were divisions among the Mughal empire, the Shii Safavid empire, and the Ottoman empire. Those who theorize about clashing civilizations conveniently ignore the fact that civilizations are not monolithic entities. During the period of the Crusades and in subsequent centuries, there were "unholy alliances" between Islam and the West—between Muslim rulers and principalities and their Christian counterparts against fellow Muslims and fellow Christians. From the sixteenth through the nineteenth centuries, various Christian powers attempted to secure the alliance of the Ottoman or Persian empires against each other.[5] And for the Muslims' part, even al-Afghani, the first theorist of Pan-Islamism, did not advocate war with the West; he was a modernist who sought Muslim unity to promote a progressive society based on science, liberty, and equality for all.

The twentieth century—humanity's bloodiest, with war and genocide taking the lives of an estimated 167 million people—not only shattered the "unity" of the West, but also swept up Muslim societies in civil wars and violent internecine conflicts.[6] Ancient divisions, conflicts, and rivalries both in the West and in Muslim societies are conveniently ignored by purveyors of the concept of a conflict among civilizations because these divisions blur or complicate the neat theories that create powerful myths about powerful enemies. But one should not forget the hostilities between Sunni and Shii Muslims, Iranians and Iraqis, Iranians and Arabs, Iranians and Turks, Iranians and the Taliban, Egypt and the Sudan, Egypt and Libya, the Sudan and Somalia, Mauritania and Morocco, Berbers and other Moroccan tribes, and Pakistan and Bangladesh, along with the tribal wars in Afghanistan and the struggles of Kurds in Iran, Turkey, and Iraq.[7]

The fact is that there is no unified "Muslim world" or unified Muslim ideology—just as there is no unified "Christian world" or unified Christian ideology, no unified "Buddhist world" or unified Buddhist ideology, no unified "Jewish world" or unified Jewish ideology. Recall that there is no single accepted Islamic theology, no single interpretation of Islamic law, no single issue around which all Muslim societies are willing to rally their people, futures, or fortunes. Even the preservation of Muslim holy places—cities like Mecca and Medina—has sometimes been a source of bitter and divisive politics among Muslims, especially the Saudi rulers and Hashemites, the former guardians of the holy places.[8]

Muslim diversity and division is a historical fact. Jill Schwedler notes, "To the extent that Islam represents a single collective identity, that identity is characterized by so many complexities and diversities as to be virtually useless analytically."[9] Putting it another way Edward W. Said asks, "How really useful is 'Islam' as a concept for understanding Morocco *and* Saudi Arabia *and* Syria *and* Indonesia? If we come to realize that, as many scholars have recently noted, Islamic doctrine can be seen as justifying capitalism as well as socialism, militancy as well as fatalism, ecumenism as well as exclusivism, we begin to sense the tremendous lag

between academic descriptions of Islam (that are inevitably cari-
catured in the media) and the particular realities to be found
within the Islamic world."[10] Clearly, it is outlandish to make
sweeping generalizations about 1.2 billion people on the basis of
their religion alone.

Paradoxically, there is agreement between those nostalgic cold
warriors who see the Green Menace replacing the Red Menace and
the militant Islamists who seek to create a worldwide Muslim
unity: both like to see Islam as a monolith. The cold warriors con-
flate militant Islamism with all of Islam, while militant Islamists
dream of a Pan-Islamic movement that will create a single Muslim
umma under a single Caliphate, or one authority, ruling from the
Atlantic Ocean to the China Sea. The latter is not a new idea—sur-
facing for the most part soon after the demise of the Ottoman
Caliphate in 1924—but the idea, whether it is considered utopian
or totalitarian, has made little headway since Prophet Muhammad's death. One cannot and should not underestimate the power
of secular states, institutions, and cultures. Nor should one ignore
the weight of history that stands firmly in the way of both a transcendent umma and a neatly delineated clash of civilizations.

Amartya Sen, the 1998 Nobel Prize winner in economics,
points out that Huntington and other clash-of-civilization theorists grossly confuse civilization with religion—and then grossly
oversimplify the world's religions. Huntington's description of
India as a "Hindu civilization" is, Sen declares, "an epistemic and
historical absurdity." India's Muslim population, Sen notes, is
greater than the combined populations of Britain and France.
There are also significant populations of Sikhs, Jains, and Budd-
hists; Christians arrived in India two centuries before they arrived

in Britain, and Jews came with the fall of Jerusalem, a thousand years ago. Sen writes:

> The reliance on civilizational partitioning fails badly. . . . First, the classifications are often based on an extraordinary epistemic crudeness and an extreme historical innocence. The diversity of traditions *within* distinct civilizations is effectively ignored, and major global interactions in science, technology, mathematics and literature over millennia are made to disappear so as to construct a parochial view of the uniqueness of Western civilization.
>
> Second, there is a basic methodological problem involved in the implicit presumption that a civilizational partitioning is the uniquely relevant distinction, and must swamp other ways of identifying people. . . .
>
> Third, there is a remarkable neglect of the role of choice and reasoning in decisions regarding what importance to attach to the membership of any particular group, or to any particular identity (among many others). By adopting a unique and allegedly predominant way of categorizing people, civilizational partitioning can materially contribute to the conflicts in the world. To deny choice when it does exist is not only an epistemic failure (a misunderstanding of what the world is like); it is also an ethical delinquency and a political dereliction of responsibility. . . .
>
> In a well-known interview, Peter Sellers once remarked: "There used to be a 'me' but I had it surgically removed." In their respective attempts to impose a single and unique identity on us, the surgical removal of the actual "me" is done by oth-

ers—the religious fundamentalist, the nationalist extremist, . . .
the sectarian provocateur. We have to resist such an imprison-
ment. We must insist upon the liberty to see ourselves as we
would choose to see ourselves. . . . The central issue, in sum, is
freedom.[11]

Stereotyping Deepens Divisions

Theories of clashing civilizations—especially when scholarly
nuances and limitations are lost in translation to slogans and
headlines—provide unwarranted support for prejudice and false
generalizations and categorizations in both Muslim and non-
Muslim societies. In the United States, for example, Paul Wyrich
and William Lind write in a booklet entitled *Why Islam Is a Threat
to America and the West* that "Islam is, quite simply, a religion of
war." Lind goes further, saying that American Muslims "should be
encouraged to leave. They are a fifth column in this country."
Columnist Ann Coulter has written, "We should invade their
countries, kill their leaders and convert them to Christianity."[12]
These sentiments are not limited to commentators in the United
States. Oriana Fallaci, the Italian journalist who lives in New York
and Italy, has written a stridently anti-Muslim book that within a
months of publication in 2002 sold more than 1.5 million copies
in Europe and 40,000 in the United States.[13] In *Rage and Pride*,
which Fallaci says she wrote in two weeks as "a scream rather than
an essay," she asserts that the Qur'an "authorizes lies, calumny,
hypocrisy."[14] Muslims, she warns, have emigrated to Western
societies, bringing fanaticism with them. "They will vex and boss
us always more and more. 'Til the point of subduing us.

Therefore, dealing with them is impossible. Attempting a dialogue, unthinkable. Showing indulgence, suicidal. And he or she who believes the contrary is a fool."[15]

Worse still are the inflammatory and widely broadcast statements of some American religious leaders. In a speech broadcast by *NBC Nightly News* in November 2001, Franklin Graham, the Christian evangelist's son, declared that Muslims pray to a "different God" and that Islam "is a very evil and wicked religion."[16] The Reverend Pat Robertson, founder of the Christian Coalition, said on CNN in February 2002, "I think people ought to be aware of what we're dealing with." Muslims "want to coexist until they can control, dominate and then, if need be, destroy." The Prophet Muhammad, Robertson said, preached hate and violence; he added, "I think Osama bin Laden is probably a very dedicated follower of Muhammad. He's done exactly what Muhammad said to do, and we disagree with him obviously, and I'm sure many moderate Muslims do as well, but you can't say the religion is a religion of peace. It's not." [17]

Speaking at the annual Southern Baptist Convention in June 2002, the Reverend Jerry Vines went so far as to call the Prophet Muhammad a "demon-possessed pedophile," saying that his twelfth wife had been a child bride. Vines is pastor of the First Baptist Church in Jacksonville, Florida, and is a past president of the convention, whose members constitute the largest (16 million) and arguably most politically active Protestant denomination in the country. Vines said that "Allah is not Jehovah" and stated that pluralism wrongly equates all religions. "Jehovah's not going to turn you into a terrorist that will try to bomb people and take the lives of thousands and thousands of people." His statement elicited criticism from both Muslim and Jewish organizations.[18]

Not only are these ministers' statements off base, they are incendiary and divisive as well. Nor do they reflect the much-hailed American values of tolerance and religious freedom. After all, if we don't practice tolerance at home, we cannot with great righteousness demand that it be practiced elsewhere. Appealing to religious agendas or religious divisions, moreover, has often led to dire consequences, including the ravages of religious wars that devastated Europe and the waves of anti-Semitism that eventually resulted in the Holocaust. It would also be as well to avoid using selected passages of ancient doctrines and texts—of Islam or any religion—to infer the views of a religion's adherents today. After all, the New Testament embraces slavery—"Slaves, obey your earthly masters with fear and trembling"—and in the Book of Joshua God commands the Israelites to kill all the Canaanites and their children. In the thirteenth century Pope Boniface VIII proclaimed that acceptance of his complete authority was "utterly necessary for the salvation of every living creature."[19]

Clearly, more education and mutual understanding are necessary. Yet this worthy goal may not be easily achieved in the current charged atmosphere surrounding any discussion of Islam. A case in point is the controversy over the University of North Carolina's requirement that incoming freshmen read *Approaching the Qur'an: The Early Revelations* by Michael Anthony Sells and write an essay on it (or write an essay on why they had chosen not to read it).[20] Bill O'Reilly, who hosts a nationally televised talk show for Fox News Network, compared the assignment to teaching

Hitler's *Mein Kampf* in 1941 and questioned the purpose of making freshmen study "our enemy's religion." As of this writing, the University of North Carolina is being sued for assigning the book, amid litigants' claims, reported in the media, that the university "indoctrinates students with deceptive claims about the peaceful nature of Islam."[21] In fact, the book does not make any general claims about Islam.

What is particularly disturbing about the debate over *Approaching the Qur'an* is that it seems to raise doubts about the role of a university, which has always been to provide a forum for the free and open discussion of ideas and precepts. (Even the U.S. Supreme Court in 1967 noted the importance of unhindered dialogue in an educational setting, calling the classroom "the marketplace of ideas.")[22] Indeed, it seems to raise doubts about the value of knowledge itself in studying orthodoxies and heterodoxies. It would seem self-evident that increased knowledge means increased understanding, not indoctrination. Shielding ourselves from the holy book of 1.2 billion Muslims is not in any way going to help begin to build a bridge from our society to others with which we have been unacquainted for far too long—or even to better acquaint ourselves with the growing Muslim community in our own country. History teaches innumerable lessons about ideas and beliefs that at first seemed frighteningly "other" and impossibly different, but with time became part of the complex tapestry of culture and practice that we now accept as an integral part of our world, even as we continue to hold to our own traditions and religions.

Religious intolerance is also a major problem among Muslims. The Foundation for the Defense of Democracies and the Saudi

Institute, two U.S.-based nonprofits, are studying hate speech by Saudi Arabian officials and institutions. Ali al-Ahmed, director of the Saudi Institute, said in a statement last year that "astonishingly, even as the Saudi government spends millions to convince Americans that they are friends and allies, they are waging a campaign based on slanders, falsehoods, intolerance and defamation." The two organizations say that the Saudi government's Institute for Islamic and Arabic Sciences in America, based in Fairfax, Virginia, and the World Assembly of Muslim Youth, in Alexandria, Virginia, promote religious intolerance against Jews, Christians, and Shii Muslims, who are a minority in Saudi Arabia. As an example of Saudi intolerance, the organizations report that the governmental institute, which is a branch of Imam Muhammad bin Sa'ud University in Riyadh, publishes books that promote intolerance. One, printed in Arabic, is entitled *A Muslim's Relations with Non-Muslims, Enmity or Friendship* . The author, a certain Abdulla Al-Tarekee, states: "The unbelievers, idolaters, and others like them must be hated and despised. . . . We must stay away from them and create barriers between us and them." He also asserts that the "Qur'an forbade taking Jews and Christians as friends, and that applies to every Jew and Christian, with no consideration as to whether they are at war with Islam or not."[23]

Saudi textbooks published by the Saudi Arabian Ministry of Education, moreover, promote intolerance, misinformation, and enmity toward the West. One text, according to a recent American study, states: "The West in particular is the source of the past and present misfortunes of the Muslim world, beginning with the Crusades, through modern Imperialism and ending in the establishment of the State of Israel. However, the West's most dangerous effect on Muslim society nowadays is its cultural and intellectual influence in various fields such as: the spread of Western practices and habits—from Western democracy to alcoholic drinks . . . Christian missionary work, Western humanitarian and medical aid, and even Western-invented computer games."[24]

Moreover, the *Protocols of the Elders of Zion* has also resurfaced in the Middle East and has been cited as factual history. This notorious anti-Semitic fabrication was first published in Russia around 1905. Supposedly a detailed plan for Jewish domination of the world, the book was used to misinform a forty-one-part "historical" drama that was produced by Egyptian state television and broadcast throughout the region in 2002.[25]

It is also clear that Muslim societies are as ignorant of our society as we are of theirs. Muslims should be informed about the evolution of our institutions, cultures, and values. This is not an easy task, especially since literacy rates are generally low in Muslim nations, allowing news, facts, and rumors to rapidly mix. How can prevailing memories of colonial rulers be dispelled, and with them, notions of conspiracy and paranoia, actual and mythical? In the former British colonies, for example, *all* Muslim problems, social and political, were often attributed to the "all-powerful, all-knowing" British empire, its agencies and agents. Following World War II, the United States seems to have inherited that mythological mantle— namely, that since we are a superpower, everything that does or does not happen in the world, especially as it affects Muslim societies, is the result of U.S. action, inaction, or acquiescence.

In this connection, therefore, it is not surprising that al-Jazeera—the satellite news outlet that claims a global television audience of 35 million Arabic speakers—broadcast a serious debate about whether the United States had staged the September 11 disaster as part of a conspiracy against Islam and China.[26] Such speculation is not confined to the media. The news service and website of Darul Uloom Deoband—as mentioned earlier, one of the largest and most influential institutions for teaching and propagating Islamic law—promoted similar rumors: "While the possibilities can not be ruled out [of] the involvement of American citizens in this act [on September 11], on the other hand a strong opinion is that the said horrible deed was hatched by the Israeli Secret Service Mosad as informed by the various sources. As [many] as four thousand Jews [were] found absent in the World Trade Center on that fateful day, moreover the assets were collected by them before the attack. What[ever] is the reason behind that, it must be investigated throughout the country."[27]

Unfortunately, paranoia and wacky conspiracy theories are hardly an exclusive staple of Muslim societies. In France, the best-selling book in early 2002—breaking the national record for first-month sales (previously held by Madonna's *Sex*)—was Thierry Meyssan's *l'Effroyable Imposture* (The horrifying fraud). He dismisses official accounts of the September 11 terrorist attacks as "a loony fable" and theorizes that the U.S. government and military executed the attacks by remote control, as part of a strategy to invade Afghanistan and Iraq. "If the energy lobby was the main beneficiary of the war in Afghanistan, the biggest victor of Sept. 11 was the military-industrial lobby," Meyssan writes. "Its wildest dreams have now been fulfilled." Nearly twenty translations of the book, including into English, were due out in late 2002.[28]

Intranational and International Dialogue

Concocting conspiracy theories and blaming external forces are easy ways to rationalize inaction and the status quo. Assuming responsibility and confronting problems head on is always difficult for rulers, regimes, and political parties, including those in Muslim countries. To analyze our mutual misconceptions, mutual stereotyping, and political and ideological differences, we must start new and honest dialogues, as well as renew support for existing dialogues.[29] This is needed not to merely affirm our respective positions, but to explore and to challenge them. Winston Churchill once joked about this deadly serious matter, "To jaw-jaw is always better than to war-war." He was right, of course.

In the United States—where we cherish religious tolerance, the concept of citizenship, and respect for ethnic heritage—domestic dialogue is necessary for engaging and understanding various Muslim communities in our midst as well as those abroad. Such dialogue should help us avoid the errors of ignorance as well as those of categorizing an entire religion and all of its adherents as our current and permanent enemy because of the acts of an individual or individual group. Otherwise, as John Esposito writes in *The Islamic Threat: Myth or Reality?* "The demonization of a great religious tradition due to the perverted actions of a minority of dissident and distorted voices remains the real threat, a threat that not only impacts on relations between the Muslim world and the West but also upon growing Muslim populations in the West itself."[30]

In Muslim societies, and within the American Muslim community, there needs to be a healthy and honest dialogue between modernists and traditionalists and between the educated secular elite and its clerical counterpart. At a time when there is a resurgence of religion and religiosity around the world, states, societies, and intellectuals ignore the importance of religion at their peril. To dismiss the role of religion in our societies is to ignore both its negative force as well as its positive contributions, including promoting and sheltering particular ethical values, as well as its role in politics and in social movements. Isolating religion, or subjecting it to benign neglect, or trying to manipulate or "purchase" the cooperation of religous leaders are not real solutions, though. Indeed, we need a dialogue that promotes understanding to prevent religion from becoming the tool of specific political parties or of secular states.

Unfortunately, many secular states have failed to pay attention to the education of religious leaders, even as their importance has grown along with religious revivals worldwide. After all, the use and abuse of religion is not just a Muslim issue, but an international one.

Global dialogues among peoples, cultures, religions, and civilizations are greatly needed. They would reveal convergances and divergances and would explore misunderstandings and genuine differences due to clashing cultural, religious, and other values and interests. In that spirit, at a 1998 United Nations discussion of these issues, Iran's president Mohammad Khatami made some welcome comments, speaking directly about the need to improve mutual knowledge and create a meaningful dialogue between American and Islamic civilizations. Khatami subsequently elaborated his views in a CNN interview: "We intend to benefit from the achievements and experiences of all civilizations, Western and non-Western, and to hold a dialogue with them. The closer the pillars and essences of these two civilizations [American and Islamic] are, the easier the dialogue would become. . . . Islam is a religion which calls all humanity, irrespective of religion or belief, to rationality and logic . . . relations among nations must be based on logic and mutual respect."[31]

Since every religion asserts its own uniqueness and claims of absolute truth and even superiority, the challenge before us all— Muslims and non-Muslims, in America and around the world—is one of understanding and accommodation: how can each group maintain and develop its own set of values and at the same time coexist and interact with other value systems, religions, and cultures? One hopes that out of dialogue will come understanding and respect, and out of respect will come tolerance.

In 1999 Pope John Paul II reached out to President Khatami and discussed ways to promote a true dialogue between Christians and Muslims. The Pope called their meeting "important and promising," and Iran's president came out of the meeting saying that all religions are "not quintessentially different."[32]

There were also many encouraging words about tolerance when more than 1,000 religious leaders from 110 countries gathered for the Millennium World Peace Summit of Religious and Spiritual Leaders at the United Nations in New York in 2000. Some excerpts from their written statements follow:[33]

Mustafa Ceric, Raisu-I-Ulama of Bosnia-Herzegovina: "The threat is not in Islam but in our spiritual disability to meet universal moral demands; evil is not in the West but in our cultural insecurity. It is time that Islam be seen as a spiritual blessing in the

West, and the West be seen as a call for an intellectual awakening in the Muslim East."

Bartholomew, Archbishop of Constantinople, New Rome, and Ecumenical Patriarch: "Whenever human beings fail to recognize the value of diversity, they deeply diminish the glory of God's creation."

Ela Gandhi, granddaughter of Mahatma Gandhi and a member of Congress in South Africa: "The different faiths are but different paths to the same end. . . . The sooner we realize this important message, the sooner we will be able to save mankind from a painful and horrendous doom—a doom of war and of natural disasters as a result of the excessive use of armaments of all types and the resultant destruction of nature."

Billy Graham, American evangelist: "Those of us who are Christians affirm that all humans are created in the image of God, and God's love extends equally to every person on earth, regardless of race, tribe or ethnic origin. . . . Every act of discrimination and racism, therefore, is wrong, and is a sin in the eyes of God."

Tenzin Gyatso, Fourteenth Dalai Lama: "Within the context of this new interdependence, self-interest clearly lies in considering the interests of others. We must develop a greater sense of universal responsibility. Each of us must learn to work not just for our own self, family, or nation, but also for the benefit of all humankind."

Israel Meir Lau, Chief Rabbi of Israel: "Judaism not only educates towards tolerance and understanding between observant and non-observant Jews, but also believes in tolerance between Jews and other religions and peoples, because all of us, all of humanity, were created in one image, the image of the Creator of the Universe. We all have one Father, one God who created us."

Njongonkulu Ndungane, Archbishop of Cape Town: "In order to live with diversity and to enjoy its riches, there is much healing to be done and, foremost, the healing of fears that lurk in the deepest recesses of our minds and hearts. We need to admit these fears in order to achieve unity in diversity and diversity in unity and to appreciate one another's giftedness. But sometimes it is our very giftedness that becomes a threat to others, and only our brokenness that unites us. . . . The only way to overcome fear is through a love that really wants the best for others. To look at those with different backgrounds and see them as God sees them. . . . There is an old saying that if you want peace, work for justice. I believe that our greatest challenge as the world's religious leaders is to consistently remind our political and business counterparts that peace is not the absence of war or conflict. It is the presence of those conditions in society that ensure basics, such as food, shelter, clothing, access to health care, clean water and education. Peace is about giving facility and nurturing a spirit of love."

Daya Mata, President and Sangmata, Self Realization Fellowship: "God is not the least bit interested in where we were born, which religion we follow, or what color our skin is. But He does care about how we behave."

Vashti M. McKenzie, Bishop, African Methodist Episcopal Church: "There are many things that divide us: different doctrines, different dogmas, different tenets, different belief systems. But if we search hard, I believe we will also find some common grounds in our differentness without violating the uniqueness of our belief systems. Now, in the 21st century, we can begin to uncover the things that bring us together rather than dwell on the things that tear us apart."

Sheng-Yen, Buddhist leader: "The best way to protect ourselves is to transform our enemies into friends. And this is at the heart of Buddhist teaching."

L. M. Singhvi, Jain scholar: "Tolerance is a state of mind, a set of norms and a pattern of behavior. It is another name for human understanding. . . . Tolerance is, in the ultimate analysis, the only way to unshackle humanity from egocentric pride and prejudice, from hatred and violence, from racial discrimination and religious fanaticism."

While most religious leaders at the peace summit addressed the need for religious tolerance, it is interesting to note that some limited their remarks to racial and ethnic intolerance. Presumably that was simply an oversight, because religious tolerance is often a critical component of racial and ethnic tolerance.

Moreover, although there have been efforts to promote religious tolerance, some efforts fall short of being inclusive of all religious ideas or modern, secular societies. Leaders of the Russian Orthodox Church and Islamic leaders, for example, have been working to improve relations by stressing their common traditions and values and experiences under Soviet oppression.[34]

A joint statement, released by Orthodox and Muslim leaders in the Republic of Tatarstan, captures this feeling: "At the close of the twentieth century, in which horrible wars (including religious ones) and persecutions for the faith have ceased, when often in the same cell were tortured the mullah and the Orthodox priest—we should draw from this the lesson of this terrible century, and enter into the twenty-first century with the clear understanding that peace on our planet is greater than thoughtless airings of the question, 'Which faith is better?'" This ecumenism, however, seems to be very limited.

One of the views shared by Muslim and Orthodox traditionalists is antagonism toward conversion carried out by proselytizing missionaries of any faith. As Talgat Tadzhuddin, Chief Mufti of European Russia, has described the "problem," missionaries "catch the souls of the young, the weak, tearing them away from their families, from a sense of love for their Fatherland, from their communities . . . the position of the Central Spiritual Administration of the Muslims of Russia . . . is in complete agreement . . . with the position of the Russian Orthodox Church." Another, unfortunate, shared view is opposition to secular and modern societies. Speaking of Muslim-Orthodox cooperation, Alekseii II, Patriarch of Moscow and All Russia, has said, "Together, we must respond to such alarming phenomena as secularization, moral crisis of society, attempts to build up a monopolar world, and to use globalization for economic, cultural, religious and information dictatorship."[35]

It is worth noting that one of the most courageous steps toward religious tolerance was taken in 1965, when, for the first time, the Vatican recognized Muslims as being part of "God's salvation plan." Despite the thousand-year delay, the Second Vatican Council's announcement, known as *Nostra Aetate*, was most welcome. Although many quarrels and hostilities have arisen between Christians and Muslims over the course of history, the council "urges all to forget the past and strive sincerely for mutual understanding. . . . All peoples of the Earth constitute a sole social community." The third clause of the declaration elaborated:

The Church looks with esteem at the Muslims who adore the only God, living and existing, merciful and omnipotent, Creator of the Heavens and the Earth, who has spoken to man. They seek to submit themselves with all their heart to God's decrees, even hidden, as did even Abraham submit himself, to whom the Islamic faith gladly refers. Although they do not recognise Jesus as God, they nevertheless venerate him as a prophet; they honour his Virgin Mother, Mary, and sometimes they even invoke her with devotion. What is more, they wait for the day of judgement when God will reward all men resurrected. Thus, they too hold in esteem moral life and pay homage to God above all with prayer, charity, and fasting.

At the time, these sentiments received a favorable response. In 1967, for example, Ahmad Omar Hashim, rector of Al-Azhar University, appealed to Muslims and Westerners to join together in seeking the common good, rather than continuing to avoid each other as a strategy to prevent conflict. "After all the suffering and indescribable affliction that humanity has gone through," he said, "we hope that humanity will be pervaded with a feeling of peace in which all religions, and principally Islam, will contribute."[36] A similarly optimistic conclusion was reached by Arnold Toynbee. In discussing the rise and fall of civilizations, he did not try to reduce the complexities to one or two factors, but rather saw historic change as an organic process involving all the variables of life. Yet he predicted that this natural process would ultimately bring about the convergence of all civilizations. "In order to save mankind we have to learn to live together in concord in spite of traditional differences of religion, class, race and civilisation. We must learn to recognise and understand the different cultural con-figurations in which our common human nature has expressed itself." This is indeed a strong challenge, but as he said, "a strong challenge often provokes a highly creative response."[37]

The time has come for the world to recognize that Jews, Chris-tians, and Muslims are the children of Abraham—and, according to the Qur'an, that our different religious communities are part of God's plan: "For every one of you [Jews, Christians, Muslims], We have appointed a path and a way. If God had willed, He would have made you but one community; but that [He has not done in order that] He may try you in what has come to you. So compete with one another in good works."[38]

The Road to Understanding

Ecumenical initiatives, off and on in recent decades, have at-tempted to promote ethnic, racial, and religious harmony. Such efforts usually have been led by religious leaders, theologians, philosophers, educators, and now and again politicians. But in modern times there have also been occasions when enlightened citizens—often individuals who believe in the unity of humanity and care of its future—have been powerful advocates for interna-tional understanding, tolerance, and peace.

One such person was Andrew Carnegie, the founder of Carne-gie Corporation of New York, where I have the privilege of serving as president. In the 1890s he became a leader of modern philan-thropy in the belief that capitalists are trustees of public wealth. He used his fortune to promote international peace and he dedicated his foundation to the premise that knowledge leads to understanding—and out of understanding comes tolerance and peaceful coexistence. He also believed that education is the true bridge, transcending all barriers, to universal progress and universal norms.

Even though Carnegie's heroic efforts failed to stop the outbreak of World War I, he still believed that there is no substitute for reason, no substitute for peace, and no substitute for progress in bringing about the betterment of humanity. If Carnegie had lived longer he certainly would have been gratified to see that his optimism, faith in reason, and belief that people do learn from experience were not completely unfounded. Today, when the possibility of international harmony seems so remote, and occasionally even hopeless, it is worth noting that sometimes the most troubled times mandate change, often with surprising results. Despite centuries of conflict, for example, the Germans and the French put aside their historical differences after World War II and worked together in laying the foundation for a new Europe. Even in the United States, in the aftermath of the Cuban missile crisis that almost started World War III, President John F. Kennedy set the pendulum swinging the other way. In a commencement address he gave at American University in 1963, he said: "Let us examine our attitude toward peace itself. Too many of us think it is impossible. Too many think it unreal. But that is a dangerous, defeatist belief. It leads to the conclusion that war is inevitable— that mankind is doomed—that we are gripped by forces we cannot control. We need not accept that view. Our problems are manmade—therefore, they can be solved by man." One solution

Kennedy announced that day was better communications: simply opening a direct telephone "hotline" between Moscow and Washington. Another, implicit in his remarks, was leadership: that day he declared a moratorium on the U.S. testing of nuclear weapons and proposed negotiations with the Soviet Union that led later the same year to the Partial Test Ban Treaty.

Present-day challenges also demand knowledge, understanding, better communications, and above all leadership. Carnegie would have been enthralled to see the major advances in the reach of education and in the dissemination of knowledge thanks to global communications technologies that have eliminated distance, and in some ways united most of humanity. At the same time, the information revolution and the associated fragmentation of knowledge have increased the necessity for new historical and sociological models, norms, and categorizations to structure our understanding of our world. But we must watch out for the pitfalls that accompany many categorizations.

I first heard such a warning in the late 1950s as a student at Stanford University, when Episcopal bishop James A. Pike stated that categorization was a sin. Around the same time, Rabbi Abraham Joshua Heschel said much the same thing. Both warned that categorization could lead, successively, to desensitization, depersonalization, and dehumanization. They reminded their audiences that builders of so-called ideal societies identify "inconvenient" or "inferior" categories of people, and justify their subjugation or "removal" by portraying them not as humans but as categories: inanimate obstacles and problems. Millions of people, who did not know they had become categories, suffered.

Both Pike and Heschel cited the twentieth century as an age of ideology and total war. The century brought the ravages of two world wars, racism, chauvinism, and xenophobia. Ideologues on the left and the right categorized and dehumanized entire peoples, classes of individuals, nations, and races. They gave the world oppression, concentration camps, "ethnic cleansing," genocide, and the Holocaust.

In the preface, I mentioned that this brief survey began as an effort to "de-categorize" Muslims living in the United States by discussing their natural racial, ethnic, cultural, regional, and religious differences. American Muslims come from different regions and different socioeconomic backgrounds, and above all else they come with rich cultural and civilizational heritages, some of them predating Islam—including those of India, China, and Persia, for example. There have always been newcomers who want to join the United States and its destiny and there always will be. One thing is clear, however: the unity and strength of our nation requires a better understanding of the pluralistic nature of our society, with its many religions, religious denominations, and ethnic and cultural legacies that contribute so much to the dynamism of America. In the spirited words of Herman Melville: "We are not a narrow tribe of men. No, our blood is that of the blood of the Amazon, made up of a thousand noble currents all pouring into one. We are not a nation so much as a world."

Yet American society has spent a long time—140 years, since Abraham Lincoln issued the Emancipation Proclamation—trying to reconcile regional, racial, ethnic, and cultural differences. Bearing in mind Lincoln's injunction "united we stand, divided we fall," we should recognize that religious freedom is one of the essential pillars of American democracy: religious tolerance cannot be rationed or given to a select group of religions but not to others. But one would hope that religious tolerance would be based on understanding, rather than on the mandate of law alone. That is why it is so important to understand Islam and its relation to other major religions, including those that in the past were only entries in dictionaries and encyclopedias and not living realities with viable communities, as they are now, in the religious haven that is America.

In this brief survey I have tried to show that Islam, like other religions, cannot be categorized or stereotyped because it is brimming with nuances, exceptions, divisions, contradictions, and ambiguities. Working for mutual understanding is a daunting challenge, but one that cannot be sidestepped. I recognize that such exhortations are easy, and what is needed is action. In this matter, we have no real choice but to learn, hold dialogues, encourage people-to-people exchanges, and engage in open and honest debates.

The new century, hopefully chastened by the bloody record of the past hundred years, will resist all ideologies—old, new, or renewed—that attempt to use religion to sow the seeds of division, hatred, and violence, be it in the form of Islamaphobia, anti-Semitism, anti-Christianity, anti-Catholicism, anti-Protestantism, anti-Hinduism, or anti-Buddhism, to name but a few. The new century should reject attempts to use religion as a tool of secular ideologies or to justify terrorism, mass murder, or assassination, often in the name of a just and merciful God. Racism, chauvinism, and xenophobia should not be given shelter by any religion.

Societies should reject the degradation of their religions. Religious intolerance is especially repugnant in the United States, which was founded on the principle of religious tolerance. It is particularly tragic when intolerance pits Muslims, Jews, and Christians against one another—members of the three Abrahamic faiths that have so much in common, including the belief that God created human beings in His own image.

The message of Saadi of Shiraz, the thirteenth-century Persian poet, is one that both Muslims and non-Muslims should take to heart:

> The children of Adam are limbs of one another
> And in their creation come from one substance
> When the world gives pain to one another
> The other members find no rest.

NOTES

Introduction

1. Fawaz A. Gerges, *America and Political Islam: Clash of Cultures or Clash of Interests?* (Cambridge University Press, 1999), pp. 23, 42.

2. Projection of the Muslim world population growth rate: U.S. Center for World Mission; growth rates for Christianity and Islam: Religious Tolerance (www.religioustolerance.org/growth_isl_chr.htm). The same U.S. Center for World Mission source, under the subhead "Growth Rates for Christianity and Islam," provides the 2023 projection in previous paragraph. Muslims as majority population: Trevor Mostyn, ed., *A Concise Guide to Islam* (Oxford University Press, 1995), p. 47, CD produced by *Prospect* magazine; John L. Esposito, *The Islamic Threat: Myth or Reality?* 3d ed. (Oxford University Press, 1999), p. 2. In India and China: Mostyn, *A Concise Guide to Islam,* p. 60. In Europe: Shireen T. Hunter, ed., *Islam, Europe's Second Religion: The New Social, Cultural, and Political Landscape* (Washington: Praeger/Center for Strategic and International Studies, 2002); John L. Esposito, "Islam as a Western Phenomenon: Implications for Europe and the United States," in Shireen T. Hunter and Huma Malik, eds., *Islam in Europe and the United States: A Comparative Perspective* (Washington: Center for Strategic and International Studies, 2002), chap. 3, p. 11, n. 1. In France, Germany, and Great Britain: Esposito, *The Islamic Threat,* p. 234. In the United States: Gustav

Niebuhr, "Studies Suggest Lower Count for Number of U.S. Muslims," *New York Times*, August 25, 2001, p. A16. In cities around the world: Esposito, "Islam as a Western Phenomenon," p. 3.

3. Lawrence H. Mamiya, "Islam in the Americas," in Azim A. Nanji, ed., *The Muslim Almanac* (Detroit: Gale Research, 1996), p. 142.

4. Survey coordinated by Hartford Institute for Religious Research, Hartford Seminary, Connecticut (April 2001) (www.cair-net.org/mosquereport).

Chapter One

1. Qur'an, Suras 3:19, 22:78, cited in Khalid Durán with Abdelwahab Hechiche, *Children of Abraham: An Introduction to Islam for Jews* (Hoboken, N.J.: Harriet and Robert Heilbrunn Institute for International Interreligious Understanding of the American Jewish Committee, 2001), p. 18. See also the companion volume: Reuven Firestone, *Children of Abraham: An Introduction to Judaism for Muslims* (Hoboken, N.J.: KTAV Publishing House, 2001).

2. Qur'an, Sura Al Baquara, verse 134, cited in the United Nations World Conference against Racism, Racial Discrimination, Xenophobia, and Related Intolerance, *Sacred Rights: Faith Leaders on Tolerance and Respect* (New York: Millwood, 2001), p. 76.

3. M. Cherif Bassiouini, *Introduction to Islam*, p. 1 (www.aeb.com/gckl/islam.htm).

4. Talbi also writes that unlike some other religions, Islam does not blame Eve for Adam's alienation from God. There was no temptress, no concept of original sin—hence, a woman did not cause the fall of humanity. There were no serpents dividing men and women. In the Qur'an, Talbi points out, God created man and woman as *zawjaha*, a couple, one entity with the same soul. Talbi questions the interpretation of a line in the Qur'an that is often used to justify men having authority over women, and he also points out there is no Qur'anic obligation for women to cover their hair. The Qur'an asks that both men and women live decent, virtuous lives and that both enjoy the same justice. See Mohamed Talbi, *Universalit'e du Coran* (Arles: Actes Sud, 2002), pp. 7, 17, 22, 44, 47, 48. For a revisionist and modern interpretation of the position of women in Islam, see Fatima Mernissi, *The Veil and the Male Elite: A Feminist Interpretation of Women's Rights in Islam* (Reading, Mass.: Addison-Wesley, 1991). See also B. F. Musallam, *Sex and Society in Islam: Birth Control before the Nineteenth Century* (Cambridge University Press, 1983), for a provocative account of the impact of birth control on the social, economic, and demographic history of Islamic society.

5. Efim A. Rezvan, "The First Qur'an," in Yuri Petrosyan and others, eds., *Pages of Perfection: Islamic Calligraphy and Miniatures from the Oriental Institute of the Russian Academy of Sciences* (St. Petersburg, N.Y.: Abbeville Press, 1996), pp. 108–09.

6. Karen Armstrong, *Islam: A Short History* (Modern Library, 2000), p. 60.

7. Trevor Mostyn, ed., *A Concise Guide to Islam* (Oxford University Press, 1995), p. 21, CD produced by *Prospect* magazine.

8. John Bowker, ed., *The Oxford Dictionary of World Religions* (Oxford University Press, 1997), p. 786.

9. Genesis 16–25; *Answering Islam: A Christian-Muslim Dialog* (http://answering-islam.org/BibleCom/gen16-3.html).

10. George B. Grose and Benjamin J. Hubbard, eds., *The Abraham Connection: A Jew, Christian and Muslim in Dialogue* (Notre Dame, Ind.: Cross Cultural Publications, 1994), pp. 2, 3.

11. Durán, *Children of Abraham*; Armstrong, *Islam*, p. 17.

12. Nishat Hasan, "Passover and Easter in Islam," *Bi-College News* (http://biconews.dyndns.org/article/articleview/321/1/18).

13. James A. Bill and John Alden Williams, *Roman Catholics and Shi'i Muslims: Prayer, Passion, and Politics* (University of North Carolina Press, 2002), p. 3.

14. Grose and Hubbard, *The Abraham Connection*, p. 21; www.answering-christianity.com/jesus_never_crucified.htm and www.answering-christianity.com/crucified.htm.

15. Durán, *Children of Abraham*, pp. 20–21.

16. Ibid., p. 210; Grose and Hubbard, *The Abraham Connection*, p. 115.

17. Bowker, *The Oxford Dictionary of World Religions*, pp. 350–52.

18. The Muslim conquests began under the second Caliph, Omar ibn Khattab, and expanded under Muawiyyah ibn Abi Sufyan of the Bani Ummayah tribe, founder of the Umayyad dynasty (661–80), who moved the Muslim capital from Medina to Damascus. See Armstrong, *Islam*.

19. Ibid., pp. xvi, 23, 29; Azim A. Nanji, ed., *The Muslim Almanac* (Detroit: Gale Research, 1996), p. 29.

20. Mostyn, *A Concise Guide to Islam*, pp. 26, 41.

21. P. J. Kavanagh, "Bywords," *Times Literary Supplement*, January 4, 2002, p. 14.

22. As an example of Islam's flexibility, when Hindus on the Indian subcontinent converted to Islam they continued to observe numerous class distinctions, ranging from noblemen to untouchables, even though such practices clearly contradicted Qur'anic injunctions for an egalitarian society.

Caste systems continue to operate in Muslim India; see Celia W. Dugger, "Indian Town's Seed Grew into the Taliban's Code," *New York Times*, February 23, 2002, p. A3. The issue of slavery also posed challenges for Islam; see G. B. Allan and Humphrey J. Fisher, *Slavery in the History of Muslim Black Africa* (New York University Press, 2001), and Ronald Segal, *Islam's Black Slaves: The Other Black Diaspora* (Farrar, Straus and Giroux, 2001).

23. Armstrong, *Islam*, p. 190.

24. Juan E. Campo, "Islam in the Middle East," in Nanji, *The Muslim Almanac*, p. 31.

25. Nanji, *The Muslim Almanac*, pp. 32, 497, 503.

26. Muslim Students Association, University of Southern California (www.usc.edu/dept/MSA/fundamentals/hadithsunnah; www.usc.edu/dept/MSA/fundamentals/hadithsunnah/scienceofhadith/asa2.html).

27. For a thorough discussion of Islam's denominations and schools of law, see Michael Cook, *Commanding Right and Forbidding Wrong in Islamic Thought* (Cambridge University Press, 2000).

28. Durán, *Children of Abraham*, pp. 26–27.

29. Mostyn, *A Concise Guide to Islam*, p. 21.

30. Nanji, *The Muslim Almanac*, pp. 34, 164, 167, 169, 171. See also Durán, *Children of Abraham*, p. 199.

31. Bill and Williams, *Roman Catholics and Shi'i Muslims*, pp. 16, 17. See also Heinz Halm, *The Fatimids and Their Traditions of Learning* (London: I. B. Tauris, 1997), p.19.

32. One radical, militant wing of Ismailis did not shy away from assassinating Sunni leaders in the eleventh century. They were called *Hashishin* (hence our word *assassin*) because, their enemies claimed, they used the drug hashish before they attacked, always with daggers and often losing their own lives in the process. Armstrong, *Islam*, pp. 69, 87; see also Bernard Lewis, "The Revolt of Islam," *New Yorker*, November 19, 2001, p. 61. Another Shii sect, the *Druze* in western Syria and Lebanon, is named after the Ismaili missionary al-Darazi, who proclaimed the divinity of the sixth Fatimid Caliph, Abu 'Ali al-Mansur al-Hakim, who ruled in Egypt in the eleventh century. The Druze, attacked by both Sunni and Shii as heretics, were so secretive that the tenets of their faith were not widely known until early in the nineteenth century. See Jane I. Smith, *Islam in America* (Columbia University Press, 1999), p. 64.

33. Durán, *Children of Abraham*, p. 28.

34. Bill and Williams, *Roman Catholics and Shi'i Muslims*, p. 57; and Ervand Abrahamian, ed., *Khomeinism: Essays on the Islamic Republic* (University of California Press, 1993).

35. Durán, *Children of Abraham*, p. 27.

36. Bill and Williams, *Roman Catholics and Shi'i Muslims*, pp. 16–25. See also Halm, *The Fatimids and Their Traditions of Learning*, p. 17, and Armstrong, *Islam*, pp. 68, 69.

37. Durán, *Children of Abraham*, p. 199.

38. John L. Esposito, *The Islamic Threat: Myth or Reality?* 3d ed. (Oxford University Press, 1999), p. 35.

39. See Durán, *Children of Abraham*, pp. 198–203.

40. Nanji, *The Muslim Almanac*, pp. 32, 273.

41. Bill and Williams, *Roman Catholics and Shi'i Muslims*, p. 20.

42. Armstrong, *Islam*, p. 200.

43. Mostyn, *A Concise Guide to Islam*, p. 21. In the eleventh and twelfth centuries, the Sunni in Afghanistan crucified Shii Ismaili "heretics," exiled Mu'tazilite scholars, and burned their philosophical and scientific books. Sunni Seljuq Turks in Central Asia also sought to stamp out science and philosophy, along with other "heresies." Mutual persecution continued unabated during the subsequent rule of the Ottomans, who oppressed the Shii, and the Safavids, who imposed Twelver Shiism as the state religion of Iran in 1501 and deported or executed the Sunni.

44. Armstrong, *Islam*, p. xvii; Nanji, *The Muslim Almanac*, p. 31.

45. W. Montgomery Watt, *The Influence of Islam on Medieval Europe* (Edinburgh University Press, 1972), cited in George Makdisi, *The Rise of Colleges: Institutions of Learning in Islam and the West* (Edinburgh University Press, 1981), p. 286. See also George Makdisi, *The Rise of Humanism in Classical Islam and the Christian West* (Edinburgh University Press, 1990); and Franz Rosenthal, *The Classical Heritage in Islam*, trans. Emile Marmorstein and Jenny Marmorstein (Routledge, 1992).

46. Nanji, *The Muslim Almanac*, pp. 31, 193.

47. Bassiouini, *Introduction to Islam*, p. 2.

48. Ismail Serageldin, "Islam, Science and Values," *International Journal of Science and Technology*, vol. 9, no. 2 (Spring 1996), pp. 100–14.

49. Halm, *The Fatimids and Their Traditions of Learning*, p. 71.

50. Randall Collins, *The Sociology of Philosophies: A Global Theory of Intellectual Change* (Harvard University Press/Belknap, 1998), p. 429.

51. For an intriguing glimpse into Andalusi history and culture, see the studies collected in Salma Khadra Jayyusi, ed., *The Legacy of Muslim Spain*, vol. 1 (Leiden: E. J. Brill, 1994), especially Mahmoud Makki, "The Political History of al-Andalus," pp. 3, 9; Robert Hillenbrand, "'The Ornament of the World': Medieval Córdoba as a Cultural Centre," pp. 112, 120, 122, 124; Pierre

Cachia, "Andalusi Belles Lettres," pp. 307, 310; and Roger Boase, "Arab Influences on European Love-Poetry," pp. 457, 459, 460.

52. Bassiouini, *Introduction to Islam,* pp. 2, 5, 8; and Pervez Hoodbhoy, *Islam and Science: Religious Orthodoxy and the Battle for Rationality* (London: Zed Books, c.1991), cited in Dennis Overbye, "How Islam Won, and Lost, the Lead in Science," *New York Times,* October 30, 2001, p. F5.

53. Jeremy Johns, "The Caliph's Circles," *Times Literary Supplement,* December 28, 2001, p. 10 (a review of Michael Brett, *The Rise of the Fatimids* [Leiden: E. J. Brill, 2002]); and Ibn al-Haytham, *The Advent of the Fatimids* (London: I. B. Tauris, 2002).

54. Nanji, *The Muslim Almanac,* pp. xxii, 31, 33, 171, 315.

55. Armstrong, *Islam,* pp. xxii, 93, 97.

56. Nanji, *The Muslim Almanac,* pp. 31, 108, 109.

57. Armstrong, *Islam,* p. 85. See also R. N. Frye, ed., *Cambridge History of Iran,* vol. 4: *From the Arab Invasion to the Seljuqs* (Cambridge University Press, 1993).

58. Halm, *The Fatimids and Their Traditions of Learning,* pp. 35, 37.

59. Esposito, *The Islamic Threat,* p. 39. See also David K. Shipler, *Arab and Jew: Wounded Spirits in a Promised Land* (Times Books, 1986), p. 11.

60. Armstrong, *Islam,* p. xxii.

61. Vartan Gregorian, *The Emergence of Modern Afghanistan: Politics of Reform and Modernization, 1880–1946* (Stanford University Press, 1969), pp. 18, 19.

62. Armstrong, *Islam,* pp. 97, 98.

63. Ibid., pp. xxvii, 97, 98, 100, 115, 130; Erik J. Zürcher, *Turkey: A Modern History* (New York: I. B. Tauris, 1998), pp. 20–21.

64. Armstrong, *Islam,* p. xxvii.

65. Some of the early imperialist policies of the colonial powers carried not only economic, but also religious and cultural agendas. The French, for example, sought to replace Islamic culture with their own by, among other measures, imposing controls on Islamic courts and suppressing many Muslim institutions. After transforming the Grand Mosque of Algiers into the Cathedral of Saint-Philippe, for example, the archbishop of Algiers announced a missionary plan to "save" Muslims from "the vices of their original religion generative of sloth, divorce, polygamy, theft, agrarian communism, fanaticism, and even cannibalism." Nanji, *The Muslim Almanac,* p. 123; Arthur Goldschmidt Jr., *A Concise History of the Middle East,* 3d ed. (Boulder, Colo.: Westview, 1988), p. 231; Esposito, *The Islamic Threat,* p. 50; Fawaz A. Gerges, *America and Political Islam: Clash of Cultures or Clash of Interests?* (Cambridge University Press, 1999).

66. Lord Kinross, *The Ottoman Centuries: The Rise and Fall of the Turkish Empire* (Morrow Quill Paperbacks, 1977); Maurice Zinkin, *Asia and the West* (Westport, Conn.: Greenwood, 1979); Zürcher, *Turkey.*

67. Bernard Lewis, "The Revolt of Islam," *New Yorker,* November 19, 2001, p. 53.

Chapter Two

1. Arnold J. Toynbee, *A Study of History,* vols. 1–10, abridged by D. C. Somervell (Oxford University Press, 1987, c.1974). See also Khwaja Masud, "A Creative Response?" *News International, Pakistan,* September 24, 2001 (www.jang.com.pk/thenews/sep2001-daily/24-09-2001/oped/o3.htm).

2. Khalid Durán with Abdelwahab Hechiche, *Children of Abraham: An Introduction to Islam for Jews* (Hoboken, N.J.: Harriet and Robert Heilbrunn Institute for International Interreligious Understanding of the American Jewish Committee, 2001), p. 46. See also Reuven Firestone, *Children of Abraham: An Introduction to Judaism for Muslims* (Hoboken, N.J.: KTAV Publishing House, 2001).

3. Karen Armstrong, *Islam: A Short History* (Modern Library, 2000) p. 6. See also Bat Ye'or, *Islam and Dhimmitude: Where Civilizations Collide* (Fairleigh Dickinson University Press, 2002); Gilles Kepel, *Jihad: The Trail of Political Islam* (Harvard University Press/Belknap, 2002); Tariq Ali, *The Clash of Fundamentalisms: Crusades, Jihads and Modernity* (London: Verso, 2002); John L. Esposito, *Unholy War: Terror in the Name of Islam* (Oxford University Press, 2002).

4. See *Encyclopedia of the Orient* (http://lexicorient.com/cgi-bin/eo-direct-frame.pl?http://i-cias.com/e.o/wahhabis.htm). On innovation, see http://islamicweb.com/beliefs/creed/wahhab.htm. On adherence to the Qur'an, see John L. Esposito and John O. Voll, *Islam and Democracy* (Oxford University Press, 1996), p. 41.

5. Over Deoband's history, more than 65,000 Islamic scholars have studied there for free, and its graduates oversee more than 40,000 *madrasas,* or traditional religious schools. In Afghanistan and Pakistan, Deobandism developed later, after the partition of the Indian subcontinent. What one sees in these countries is not the evolved form of Indian Deobandism, but instead the orthodox form of Wahhabi Islam with the Taliban's version of Islam grafted onto it. This highly ideological form of Islam was taught in religious schools, including one near Peshawar that trained many of the top Taliban leaders. See Kartikeya Sharma, "Scholar's Getaway," *The Week,* July 1, 2001 (www.the-week.com/21jul01/life8.htm). See also Barbara D. Metcalf,

"'Traditionalist' Islamic Activism: Deoband, Tablighis, and Talibs," Social Science Research Council (www.ssrc.org/sept11/essays/metcalf_text_only. htm); and Celia W. Dugger, "Indian Town's Seed Grew into the Taliban's Code," New York Times, February 23, 2002, p. A3.

6. Azim A. Nanji, ed., The Muslim Almanac (Detroit: Gale Resesarch, 1996), pp. 39, 434.

7. John L. Esposito, The Islamic Threat: Myth or Reality? 3d ed. (Oxford University Press, 1999), pp. 53–54; see also Majid Fakhry, A History of Islamic Philosophy, 2d ed. (Columbia University Press, 1987), p. 399.

8. Armstrong, Islam, p. xxviii.

9. Albert Hourani, Arabic Thought in the Liberal Age (Oxford University Press, 1970), p. 109; and Esposito, The Islamic Threat, pp. 53, 54.

10. Sayyid Jamal ad-Din al-Afghani, "Lecture on Teaching and Learning," delivered at the Albert Hall, Calcutta, November 8, 1882, as reprinted in Nikki R. Keddie, An Islamic Response to Imperialism (University of California Press, 1968), p. 107.

11. Vartan Gregorian, The Emergence of Modern Afghanistan: Politics of Reform and Modernization, 1880–1946 (Stanford University Press, 1969), pp. 163, 176.

12. Armstrong, Islam, p. 151.

13. In 2002, for example, Wafa Fageeh, a professor at Abdulaziz University, performed the world's first transplant of a human uterus with her team at the King Fahad Hospital and Research Center in Jiddah, Saudi Arabia. See Emma Ross, "First Human Uterus Transplant Performed by Saudi Doctors," Associated Press, March 7, 2002 (www.canoe.ca/Health0203/07_uterus-ap.html).

14. Nanji, The Muslim Almanac, pp. 416–17.

15. Randall Collins, The Sociology of Philosophies: A Global Theory of Intellectual Change (Harvard University Press/Belknap, 1998), p. 449. See also Ian Buruma, Inventing Japan (Random House, 2003).

16. Pervez Hoodbhoy, Islam and Science: Religious Orthodoxy and the Battle for Rationality (London: Zed Books, c.1991), cited in Dennis Overbye, "How Islam Won, and Lost, the Lead in Science," New York Times, October 30, 2001, p. F5.

17. In Islamabad, a professor was sentenced to death in 2000 after some medical students accused him of blasphemy. Akbar Ahmed and Lawrence Rosen, "Islam, Academe, and Freedom of the Mind," Chronicle of Higher Education, November 2, 2001, p. B11.

18. United Nations Development Program and the Arab Fund for Economic and Social Development, "The Arab Human Development Report

2002" (www.undp.org/rbas/ahdr); see also Thomas L. Friedman, "Arabs at the Crossroads," *New York Times*, July 2, 2002, p. A23.

Chapter Three

1. www.salaam.co.uk.

2. Azim A. Nanji, ed., *The Muslim Almanac* (Detroit: Gale Resesarch, 1996), p. 68; see also Muslim Students Association, University of Southern California (www.usc.edu/dept/MSA/history/chronology/century20.html); and www.salaam.co.uk.

3. John L. Esposito, *The Islamic Threat: Myth or Reality?* 3d ed. (Oxford University Press, 1999), pp. 65, 66.

4. John L. Esposito and John O. Voll, *Islam and Democracy* (Oxford University Press, 1996), p. 41.

5. Jillian Schwedler, "Islamic Identity: Myth, Menace, or Mobilizer?" *SAIS Review*, vol. 21, no. 2 (Summer–Fall 2001), p. 7.

6. www.arab.de/arabinfo/libya-government.htm.

7. Esposito, *The Islamic Threat*, p. 64.

8. Stanley Wolpert, *Jinnah of Pakistan* (Oxford University Press, 1984), pp. 332, 339.

9. The Nuclear Threat Initiative (www.nti.org/e_research/e1_india_1.html).

10. Ali A. Mazrui, "The Nuclear Option and International Justice," in Nimat Hafez Barazangi, ed., *Islamic Identity and the Struggle for Justice* (University Press of Florida, 1996), p. 102. Mazrui cites C. Smith and Shyam Bhatia, "How Dr. Khan Stole the Bomb for Islam," *Observer* (London), December 9, 1979.

11. Daniel Pipes, "U.S. Warmed to Zia, as It Must to Successor," *Los Angeles Times*, August 18, 1988 (http://danielpipes.org/article/182). See also BBC, "Pakistan and the Northern Alliance" (www.punjabilok.com/america_under_attack/pakistan_northern_alliance.htm); Reuel Marc Gerecht, "Pakistan's Taliban Problem," *Weekly Standard*, November 5, 2001; and American Enterprise Institute for Public Policy Research (www.aei.org/ra/ragere011105.htm).

12. Mazrui, "The Nuclear Option and International Justice," p. 114.

13. As for "rectifying injustices," the new Iranian government, dominated by conservative clerics, made "corrections" according to its own narrow agenda. It declared war against liberals, radicals, and some minorities, including the followers of Bahai World Faith. The Bahai, whose members believe in

the integration of all world religions, were accused of having collaborated with the Shah, Israel, and the United States. Their assets were seized, and one leader, Ayatullah Sadduqi, declared the Bahai to be *mahdur ad-damm*, or "those whose blood may be shed." Robert E. Burns, *The Wrath of Allah* (Houston: A. Ghosh, 1994) (www.hraic.org/some_islamic_history.html).

14. Nanji, *The Muslim Almanac*, p. 43; Bernard Lewis, "The Revolt of Islam," *New Yorker*, November 19, 2001, p. 54.

15. Andrew Rippin and Jan Knappert, eds., *Textual Sources for the Study of Islam* (University of Chicago Press, 1986), p. 192. For a more detailed look at Iran in this period, see also Roy P. Mottahedeh, *The Mantle of the Prophet: Religion and Politics in Iran* (Pantheon, 1986).

16. Seymour M. Hersh, "King's Ransom," *New Yorker*, November 26, 2001.

Chapter Four

1. Jillian Schwedler, "Islamic Identity: Myth, Menace, or Mobilizer?" *SAIS Review*, vol. 21, no. 2 (Summer–Fall 2001), pp. 1, 5, 7.

2. The Islamic Salvation Front's victories in Algeria resulted from winning a plurality of votes: only 3.25 million of 13 million votes cast. It is worth noting that only half of the Islamic Salvation Front's supporters approved of the establishment of an "Islamic state," according to a survey at the time. Outside Iran, no Islamist party has won a majority of votes in any national election. Even though Islamist parties probably attract many "protest" votes against mainstream parties, they have not received more than 30 percent of the vote in internationally monitored elections in nations such as Yemen, Pakistan, Turkey, and Jordan. Max Rodenbeck, "Is Islamism Losing Its Thunder?" *Washington Quarterly*, vol. 21, no. 2 (Spring 1998), p. 177.

However, in November 2002 a Turkish party with some Islamist and traditionalist roots, the Justice and Development Party, easily defeated the existing coalition government by winning 34.2 percent of the vote, or 363 of the 550 seats in parliament—just four seats less than needed to rewrite the nation's constitution. But the party's leader, Recep Tayyip Erdogan, has distanced it from other religious-based parties that have been banned in Turkey and has countered secular concerns by saying that the party supports human rights, including freedom of religion. BBC News World Edition, "Turkey's Old Guard Routed in Elections," November 4, 2002 (http://news.bbc.co.uk/2/hi/europe/2392717.stm and http://news.bbc.co.uk/2/hi/europe/2125827.stm).

3. Azim A. Nanji, ed., *The Muslim Almanac* (Detroit: Gale Research, 1996), pp. 41, 42.

4. Karen Armstrong, *Islam: A Short History* (Modern Library, 2000), p. 156.

5. Neil MacFarquhar, "Egyptian Group Patiently Pursues Dream of Islamic State," *New York Times*, January 20, 2002, p. 3; also John L. Esposito, *The Islamic Threat: Myth or Reality?* 3d ed. (Oxford University Press, 1999), pp. 129, 133.

6. Nanji, *The Muslim Almanac*, p. 436; MacFarquhar, "Egyptian Group Patiently Pursues Dream of Islamic State," p. 3.

7. Derek Hopwood, "The Culture of Modernity in Islam and the Middle East," in John Cooper, Ronald Nettler, and Mohamed Mahmoud, eds., *Islam and Modernity: Muslim Intellectuals Respond* (New York: I. B. Tauris, 2000), p. 7.

8. Robert Irwin, "Is This the Man Who Inspired Bin Laden?" *Guardian* (London), November 1, 2001 (www.guardian.co.uk/g2/story/0,3604,584478, 00.html). See also Malise Ruthven, *A Fury for God: The Islamist Attack on America* (London: Granta, 2002); Olivier Roy, *The Failure of Political Islam* (Harvard University Press, 1994); and Paul Berman, "The Philosopher of Islamic Terror," *New York Times Magazine*, March 23, 2003.

9. Robert Irwin, writing in the *Guardian,* connects Qutb with his disciples in the Taliban and al-Qaeda: "Qutb seems to have rejected all kinds of government, secular and theocratic, and on one reading at least, he seems to advocate a kind of anarcho-Islam. On the one hand, his writings have exercised a formative influence on the Taliban, who, under the leadership of the shy, rustic Mullah Omar, seem to have been concentrating on implementing the Shari'a in one country under the governance of the Mullahs. On the other hand, Qutb's works have also influenced [al-Qaida], which, under the leadership of the flamboyant and camera-loving Bin Laden, seems to aim at a global jihad that will end with all men under direct, unmediated rule of Allah. In the context of that global programme, the destruction of the twin towers, spectacular atrocity though it was, is merely a by-blow in [al-Qaida's] current campaign. Neither the U.S. nor Israel is Bin Laden's primary target—rather it is Bin Laden's homeland, Saudi Arabia. The corrupt and repressive royal house, like the Mongol Ilkhanate of the 14th century, is damned as a Jahili scandal. Therefore, [al-Qaida's] primary task is to liberate the holy cities of Mecca and Medina from their rule. Though the current policy of the princes of the Arabian peninsula seems to be to sit on their hands and hope that [al-Qaida] and its allies will pick on someone else first, it is unlikely that they will be so lucky." Irwin, "Is This the Man Who Inspired Bin Laden?" See also Ruthven, *A Fury for God.*

10. Ibrahim M. Abu-Rabi, *Intellectual Origins of Islamic Resurgence in the Modern Arab World* (State University of New York Press, 1996), pp. 64, 70, 74.

See also Abdel Salam Sidahmed and Anoushiravan Ehteshami, *Islamic Fundamentalism* (Boulder, Colo.: Westview, 1996), pp. 166, 167, 168; and Mac-Farquhar, "Egyptian Group Patiently Pursues Dream of Islamic State," p. 3.

11. Family Education Network (www.teachervision.com/lesson-plans/lesson-6984.html).

12. http://rawasongs.fancymarketing.net.rules.htm; www.globalpolicy.org/security/issues/afghan/2001/0306puni.htm; Kenneth Cooper, "Afghanistan's Taliban: Going Beyond Its Islamic Upbringing," *Washington Post*, March 9, 1998; Kathy Gannon, "What Manner of Muslims Are Taliban?" Associated Press, September 19, 2001; http://mosaic.echonyc.com/~onissues/su98goodwin.html; and Family Education Network (www.teachervision.com/lesson-plans/lesson-6984.htm).

13. Rodenbeck, "Is Islamism Losing Its Thunder?" p. 177.

14. Mary Ann Weaver, "The Real Bin Laden," *New Yorker*, January 24, 2000.

15. Shireen T. Hunter, "Islam, Modernization and Democracy: Are They Compatible?" *CSIS Insights* (March–April 2002).

16. Afghanistan Atlas Project, "Where Did the Taliban Come From?" University of Nebraska at Omaha (www.unomaha.edu/afghanistan_atlas/talhis.html).

17. "The Challenge for Moderate Islam," *Economist*, June 22, 2002, p. 37.

18. John L. Esposito and John O. Voll, "Islam and Democracy," *Humanities* (November–December 2001), p. 22.

19. Merle C. Ricklefs, "Liberal, Tolerant Islam Is Fighting Back," *International Herald Tribune*, April 27, 2002.

20. Gilles Kepel, *Jihad: The Trail of Political Islam* (Harvard University Press/Belknap, 2002).

21. See also the following reviews of Kepel's book: "Wave of the Past," *Economist*, June 1, 2002; Fred Halliday, "The Fundamental Things," *Los Angeles Times*, June 23, 2002, p. R4; Robin Wright, "Mosque and State," *New York Times*, May 26, 2002, sec. 7, p. 10.

22. Central Intelligence Agency, *World Factbook* (2001) (www.cia.gov/cia/publications/factbook/geos/iz.html); Hugh Pope, "Iraq's Hussein Emphasizes Islamic Identity to Shore Up Legitimacy," *Wall Street Journal*, April 29, 2002, p. A14.

23. Pope, "Iraq's Hussein Emphasizes Islamic Identity to Shore Up Legitimacy," p. A14.

24. Olivier Roy, "*Qibla* and the Government House: The Islamist Networks," *SAIS Review*, vol. 21, no. 2 (Summer–Fall 2001), p. 53; Shireen T. Hunter, "Religion, Politics and Security in Central Asia," *SAIS Review*, vol. 21, no. 2 (Summer–Fall 2001), p. 68.

25. When Islamists condemn the "West's indifference" toward the plight of Muslims, they conveniently ignore American and European efforts in Chechnya, Bosnia, and Kosovo. They also ignore U.S. support of Afghans in their struggle with the Soviet Union and the U.S.- led international coalition that rescued Kuwait, with its largely traditionalist Muslim population, from the harsh grip of secular, socialist Iraq.

26. President George W. Bush, June 24, 2002, *PBS Online NewsHour* (www. pbs.org/newshour/bb/middle_east/jan-june02/bush_speech_6-24. html).

27. See International Crisis Group, *Middle East Endgame I: Getting to a Comprehensive Arab-Israeli Peace Settlement, Middle East Endgame II: How a Comprehensive Israeli-Palestinian Peace Settlement Would Look*, and *Middle East Endgame III: Israel, Syria and Lebanon—How Comprehensive Peace Settlements Would Look* (July 16, 2002); Yohanan Manor, "The Future of Peace in the Light of School Textbooks" (Nice: Center for Monitoring the Impact of Peace, May 2002).

28. The terrorists who participated in the September 11 attacks, for example, were mostly well-educated men from middle-class families in Saudi Arabia. Recent studies also confirm that relatively high levels of education and income are common among members of terrorist organizations in many parts of the world, including Hezbollah in Palestine, Gush Emunim in Israel, the Japanese Red Army, and Italy's Red Brigades. Alan Krueger and Jitka Maleckova, "Education, Poverty, Political Violence and Terrorism: Is There a Causal Connection?" May 2002 (www.wws.princeton.edu/~rpds/education. pdf). See also Robert J. Barro, "The Myth That Poverty Breeds Terrorism," *BusinessWeek*, June 10, 2002, p. 26.

Chapter Five

1. John L. Esposito and John O. Voll, *Islam and Democracy* (Oxford University Press, 1996), pp. 3, 193.

2. Shireen T. Hunter, "Islam, Modernization and Democracy: Are They Compatible?" *CSIS Insights* (March–April 2002).

3. Christopher Reardon, "Islam and the Modern World," *Ford Foundation Report*, vol. 33, no. 1 (Winter 2002), pp. 19, 20.

4. Jesse J. DeConto, "Professor Disputes Four Myths about Islam," *Portsmouth Herald* (N.H.), October 6, 2001.

5. "The Challenge for Moderate Islam," *Economist*, June 22, 2002, p. 37.

6. Benito Mussolini, "What Is Fascism? 1932," excerpt from the *Italian Encyclopedia*, Modern History Sourcebook (www.fordham.edu/halsall/mod/mussolini-fascism.html).

7. Abu'l A'la Mawdudi, "Political Theory of Islam," in Khurshid Ahmad, ed., *Islam: Its Meaning and Message* (London: Islamic Council of Europe, 1976), pp. 160–61, cited in Esposito and Voll, *Islam and Democracy,* p. 24.

8. Robert Wuthnow, ed., *Encyclopedia of Politics and Religion* (Washington: Congressional Quarterly Press, 1998), pp. 383–93 (www.cqpress.com/context/articles/epr_islam.html). Quote is from Ishaq Musa'ad and Kenneth Cragg, eds., *Risalat at-Tawhid (The Message of Unity)* (London: Allen and Unwin, 1966); see Ted Thornton and Dick Schwingel, Northfield Mount Hermon School website on the Islamic Middle East (www.nmhschool.org/tthornton/muhammad_abduh).

9. www.nmhschool.org/tthornton/muhammad_abduh.htm.

10. Reardon, "Islam and the Modern World," p. 19.

11. John Cooper, Ronald Nettler, and Mohamed Mahmoud, eds., *Islam and Modernity: Muslim Intellectuals Respond* (New York: I. B. Tauris, 2000), p. 9, see also chap. 6. For an in-depth exposition of Mohamed Talbi's philosophy and writings on the Qur'an and God's alliance with man, the Qur'an and history, Islam and liberty, the Bible and the Qur'an, see Mohamed Talbi and Gwendoline Jarczyk, *Penseur libre en Islam: Un intellectuel musulman dans la Tunisie de Ben Ali* (Paris: Albin Michel, 2002).

12. Mohamed Charfi, *Islam et liberté: La malentendu historique* (Paris: Albin Michel, 1998).

13. Mohammed Arkoun, *Lectures du Coran,* 2d ed. (Tunis: G.-P. Maisonneuve et Larose, 1991); Arkoun, *Rethinking Islam: Common Questions, Uncommon Answers* (Boulder, Colo.: Westview, 1993); Arkoun, *La pensée arabe* (Paris: PUF, 1996). Abdou Filali-Ansary, *L'Islam est-il hostile à la laïcité?* (Morocco: Le Fennec, 1996; Sindbad, 2002); Filali-Ansary, *Par souci de clarté: A propos des sociétés musulmanes contemporaines* (Morocco: Le Fennec, 2001). See also Abdou Filali-Ansary, *Réformer L'Islam? Une Introduction aux Débats Contemporains* (Paris: La Découverte, 2003).

14. Abdolkarim Soroush, *Reason, Freedom, and Democracy in Islam* (Oxford University Press, 2000), pp. 128, 132. For further exploration of the writings of Soroush, see Cooper, Nettler, and Mahmoud, *Islam and Modernity,* chap. 2.

15. Fatima Mernissi, *The Veil and the Male Elite: A Feminist Interpretation of Women's Rights in Islam* (Reading, Mass.: Addison-Wesley, 1991).

16. Esposito and Voll, *Islam and Democracy,* p. 29.

17. Altaf Gauhar, "Islam and Secularism," in Altaf Gauhar, ed., *The Challenge of Islam* (London: Islamic Council of Europe, 1978), p. 307, cited in Esposito and Voll, *Islam and Democracy,* p. 29.

18. John L. Esposito and John O. Voll, "Islam and Democracy," *Humanities* (November–December 2001), p. 22. See chap. 4, n. 2 (p. 146) above, on elections in Turkey.

19. Ariel Swartley, "The Persian Poet's Old Verse Speaks to the New Age Heart," *Los Angeles Times Magazine*, October 1, 2001, p. 166. See also www.khamush.com/poems.html.

20. Seymour Hersh, "The Getaway: Questions Surround a Secret Pakistani Airlift," *New Yorker*, January 28, 2001, p. 39.

21. Jonathan Rauch, "Islam Has Been Hijacked, Only Muslims Can Save It," *National Journal*, October 13, 2001.

22. "Hamas Vows to Avenge Death of Bombmaker," *USA Today*, July 1, 2002 (www.usatoday.com/news/world/2002/07/01/hamas-revenge.htm# more). In Palestine there is real soul searching as to the best means of resisting the Israeli occupation and whether suicide bombing as a kind of "resistance of last resort" is counterproductive. Surveys indicate that about half the Palestinian population supports suicide bombing, and a much larger majority opposes arresting Islamists who organize the bombings. The tide may be turning, however slowly. In June 2002, a group of fifty-five Palestinian politicians and scholars ran a newspaper advertisement for several days that called for reconsidering "military operations that target civilians in Israel." It asked for a halt in "pushing our youth to carry out these operations." The letter did not condemn the suicide missions but argued that they were not "producing any results except confirming the hatred . . . between the two peoples" and jeopardizing the "possibility that two peoples will live side by side in peace in two neighboring states." Within a few days, more than 500 had signed on to the statement, some via the Internet; a rebuttal gained about 150 signatures. James Bennet, "Gingerly, Arabs Question Suicide Bombings," *New York Times*, July 3, 2002, p. A1.

23. Susan Sachs, "Where Muslim Traditions Meet Modernity," *New York Times*, December 17, 2001, p. B1.

24. Bat Ye'or, *Islam and Dhimmitude: Where Civilizations Collide* (Fairleigh Dickinson University Press, 2002), p. 385.

25. Azim A. Nanji, ed., *The Muslim Almanac* (Detroit: Gale Research, 1996), p. 387.

26. "Some Progress for Turkish Women," editorial, *New York Times*, June 19, 2002.

27. "Gender Plays an Important Role," *Geneva News* (www.genevanews.com/gnir/html/Archives/199710/CoverStory9710.html).

28. Changing a tradition of intolerance can be difficult. In Saudi Arabia, the government has introduced plans to remove intolerant passages from

textbooks. As a result, there has been "a lively debate in Saudi newspapers, with prominent conservative clergyman Sheik Saleh al-Fawzan, the author of many texts used in Saudi religious curricula, and Education Minister Mohammed Ahmed Rasheed trading insults." James M. Dorsey, "Saudi Leader Seeks to Rein in Clergy," *Wall Street Journal*, March 14, 2002, p. A9.

29. Susan Sachs, "In One Muslim Land, an Effort to Enforce Lessons of Tolerance," *New York Times*, December 16, 2001, p. A4.

30. Ye'or, *Islam and Dhimmitude*, pp. 384–85.

31. Ibid.

Chapter Six

1. George Will, "Take Time to Understand Mideast Asia," *Washington Post*, October 29, 2001.

2. Public Agenda, "For Goodness' Sake: Why So Many Want Religion to Play a Greater Role in American Life," survey of 1,507 adults conducted November 4–25, 2000 (www.publicagenda.org).

3. National Commission on Asia in the Schools, "Asia in the Schools: Preparing Young Americans for Today's Interconnected World," *Asia Society*, June 20, 2001.

4. Samuel P. Huntington, *The Clash of Civilizations and the Remaking of World Order* (Simon and Schuster, 1996). See also Samuel P. Huntington, "The Age of Muslim Wars," *Newsweek*, special edition, December 2001– February 2002, pp. 7, 29.

5. For example, after Philip II of Spain conquered Portugal, his archenemy, Queen Elizabeth I of England, opened diplomatic negotiations with the Ottoman empire. She called Philip "that arch-idolater" and befriended Sultan Murad as "the unconquered and most puissant defender of the true faith against the idolaters." See Lord Kinross, *The Ottoman Centuries: The Rise and Fall of the Turkish Empire* (Morrow Quill, 1977), pp. 321, 324. For a further discussion of Muslim-Christian alliances, see Fawaz A. Gerges, *America and Political Islam: Clash of Cultures or Clash of Interests?* (Cambridge University Press, 1999), chap. 3.

6. Zbigniew Brzezinski, *Out of Control: Global Turmoil on the Eve of the 21st Century* (Charles Scribner's Sons, 1993).

7. For a variety of perspectives on Islam's diversity, see Nissim Rejwan, ed., *The Many Faces of Islam: Perspectives on a Resurgent Civilization* (University Press of Florida, 2000).

8. See Elaine Sciolino, "Where the Prophet Trod, He Begs, Tread Lightly," *New York Times*, February 15, 2002, p. A4. For a discussion of tolerance in

Islam, see also Khaled Abou El Fadl, ed., *The Place of Tolerance in Islam* (Boston: Beacon Press, 2002).

9. Jillian Schwedler, "Islamic Identity: Myth, Menace, or Mobilizer?" *SAIS Review,* vol. 21, no. 2 (Summer–Fall 2001), p. 7.

10. Edward W. Said, *Covering Islam: How the Media and the Experts Determine How We See the Rest of the World,* rev. ed. (Vintage Books, 1997 [1981]), p. lv.

11. Amartya Sen, "Civilizational Imprisonments: How to Misunderstand Everybody in the World," *New Republic,* June 10, 2002, pp. 28–33.

12. Nicholas D. Kristof, "Bigotry in Islam—and Here," *New York Times,* July 9, 2002, p. A21.

13. George Gurley, "The Rage of Oriana Fallaci," *New York Observer,* January 27, 2003, p. 1.

14. Oriana Fallaci, *Rage and Pride* (New York: Rizzoli International, 2002). See "Europe: How to Accommodate the Muslims Among Us," *The Week,* July 5, 2002, p. 12.

15. Oriana Fallaci, "How the West Was Won—And How It Will Be Lost," *American Enterprise* (January–February 2003), p. 47. This is an excerpt from her October 22, 2002, speech at the American Enterprise Institute, in which she quoted her book.

16. "Graham on Islam: Should a Religion Be Blamed for Its Adherents' Evil Acts?" *Charlotte Observer,* November 20, 2001, p. 14A.

17. "Robertson Defends Comments about Islam," February 24, 2002 (www.cnn.com/2002/allpolitics/02/24/robertson.islam/index.html); and "Robertson Stands behind Remarks on Islam, February 25, 2002 (www.cnn.com/2002/US/02/25/robertson.islam.cnna/index.html). See also "Robertson Insists Islam Is Dangerous," *Philadelphia Inquirer,* February 25, 2002, p. A4.

18. Susan Sachs, "Baptist Pastor Attacks Islam, Inciting Cries of Intolerance," *New York Times,* June 15, 2002, p. A10.

19. Thomas Cahill, "The One True Faith: Is It Tolerance?" *New York Times,* February 3, 2002, p. A1; Kristof, "Bigotry in Islam," p. A21.

20. Michael Anthony Sells, *Approaching the Qur'an: The Early Revelations* (Ashland, Ore.: White Cloud Press, 1999).

21. Alan Cooperman, "N.C. College's Summer Read Draws Heat," *Philadelphia Inquirer,* August 8, 2002, p. A1; "Book Value: Lawsuit against Koran Assignment Ignores the Mission of the Universities," editorial, *Philadelphia Inquirer,* August 8, 2002, p. A18; Michael Sells, "Understanding, not Indoctrination," *Washington Post,* August 8, 2002, p. A17.

22. *Keyishian v. Board of Regents of the State University of New York,* 385 U.S. 589 (1967), cited in Vartan Gregorian, *Higher Education's Accomplishments and*

Challenges, Davis, Markert, Nickerson Lecture on Academic and Intellectual Freedom (University of Michigan Law School, September 11, 2001), pp. 5–6.

23. Saudi Institute and Foundation for the Defense of Democracies, "Saudis Spread Hate Speech in U.S." (www.saudiinstitute.org/hate.htm and www.defenddemocracy.org/templ/Display.cfm?id=174&Sub=182). The boards of directors and advisers of the Foundation for the Defense of Democracies includes prominent politicians, former government officials, and policy experts, including Jack Kemp, Newt Gingrich, James Woolsey, and Jean Kirkpatrick.

24. Arnon Groiss, comp., trans., ed., "The West, Christians and Jews in Saudi Arabian Schoolbooks" (New York: Center for Monitoring the Impact of Peace and the American Jewish Committee, January 2003), abridged version, p. 11.

25. AntiDefamation League, "*The Protocols of the Elders of Zion*: The Renaissance of anti-Semitic Hate Literature in the Arab and Islamic World" (www.adl.org/css/proto_intro.asp).

26. "Roundtable," *Prospect,* November 2001, p. 21.

27. http://darululoom-deoband.com/english/index.htm.

28. Thierry Meyssan, *l'Effroyable Imposture* (Paris: Carnot, 2002). See also Bruce Crumley, "Conspiracy Theory," *Time Europe,* May 20, 2002.

29. A. Kamal Aboulmagd and others, *Crossing the Divide: Dialogue among Civilizations,* United Nations Year of Dialogue among Civilizations (Seton Hall School of Diplomacy, 2001); "Crossing the Divide: Dialogue among Civilizations," *Global Dialogue,* vol. 2, no. 1 (Winter 2001); Roald Sagdeev and Susan Eisenhower, eds., *Islam and Central Asia* (Washington: Center for Political and Strategic Studies, 2000).

30. John L. Esposito, *The Islamic Threat: Myth or Reality?* 3d ed. (Oxford University Press, 1999), p. xiii.

31. Transcript of Interview with Iranian President Mohammad Khatami, January 7, 1998 (www.cnn.com/WORLD/9801/07/iran/interview.html).

32. James A. Bill and John Alden Williams, *Roman Catholics and Shi'i Muslims: Prayer, Passion, and Politics* (University of North Carolina Press, 2002), pp. 1, 2.

33. Millennium World Peace Summit of Religious and Spiritual Leaders, *Sacred Rights: Faith Leaders on Tolerance and Respect* (Millwood, 2001), compiled (with contributions from attendees) in cooperation with the Office of the United Nations High Commissioner for Human Rights, Bawa Jain, secretary general.

34. Nikolas K. Gvosdev, "When Mullahs and Metropolitans Meet: The Emerging Orthodox-Islamic Consensus in Eurasia," *Orthodox News,* vol. 3, no. 7 (May 2, 2001).

35. Ibid.

36. Vartan Gregorian, "Dialogue among Civilizations: A New Paradigm," presentation at the United Nations Headquarters, New York, May 6, 1999.

37. Khwaja Masud, "A Creative Response?" *News International, Pakistan*, September 24, 2001 (www.jang.com.pk/thenews/sep2001-daily/24-09-2001/oped/o3.htm).

38. Qur'an, Sura 5:48, as translated in Abdulaziz Sachedina, *Islamic Roots of Democratic Pluralism* (Oxford University Press, 2001), p. 63.

INDEX

toward, 106, 119; punishment, 6
North Carolina, University of 117–18
Nowbowat, 7
Number of Muslims, 1, 22

Obaid, Thoraya, 54
Oil economy, 64
O'Reilly, Bill, 117–18
Organization of the Islamic
Conference, 80
Original sin, 10–11
Origins and early development, 5–6,
11–14
Ottoman empire, 33, 35–38; World
War I, 57–58

Pahlavi, Reza Shah, 59
Pakistan, 52, 63–64, 93, 94, 100; and
Kashmir, 63, 64, 85–88; nuclear
arsenal, 65–66; Soviet invasion of
Afghanistan, 67–68
Palestine, 60, 85, 88
Paradise, 19
Persian empire, 12, 16
Persian Gulf war, 62, 84
Pike, James A., 132
Pillars of Faith, 7–8, 35
Poitiers, Battle of, 11
Political context: civil rights, 55–56;
decline of Islamic empires, 37–38;
early development of Islam, 12;
Golden Age, 31–32; Islamic parties,
80–81; Islamist movements, 73–74,
75, 80–81, 100; manipulation of
religion, 98; post–World War II
Arab states, 60–62; separation of
mosque and state, 41–42, 101;
spiritual leadership, 14. See also
Democratic practice

Poverty, 8, 55
Prayer, 7–8
Productivity, 55
Prophets, 6, 7, 10
Protocols of the Elders of Zion, 120
Publishing, 54
Punishment, 6, 12–13

al-Qaida, 78, 79
Qasim Nanauti, Maulana
Mohammed, 44
Qur'an: in Islamic law, 8–9, 22; Jesus,
10; modernist interpretation, 96; in
Mu'tazilist theology, 16; on
nonbelievers, 12–13; origins, 6, 7,
18–19; significance, 6–7; structure,
6; translations, 7; Western
understanding, 117–18
Qureish tribe, 5
Qutb, Sayyid, 78

Radcliffe, Cyril, 63
Rahman, Marghboor, 44
al-Rahman III, Abd, 31–32
Ramadan, 6, 8
Rationalism, 16, 22, 25; in Islam, 95;
religious faith and, 91–92, 95, 97
Revivalism: goals, 68–70; historical
development, 70–72; Islamism and,
72; origins, 69
Richard I, 33
Rida, Rashid, 96
Robertson, Pat, 116
Rumi, Jalal al-Din, 100
Rushdie, Salman, 18
Russia, 36, 37, 38
Russian Federation, 2
Russian Orthodox Church, 127–28

Saadi of Shiraz, 135